The Evolution Dialogues

SCIENCE, CHRISTIANITY, AND THE QUEST FOR UNDERSTANDING

by Catherine Baker

James B. Miller, Editor

Program of Dialogue on Science, Ethics, and Religion
American Association for the Advancement of Science

ADVANCING SCIENCE, SERVING SOCIETY

Printed in the United States of America

International Standard Book Number: 0-87168-709-7

Copyright ©2006
American Association for the Advancement of Science
1200 New York Avenue, NW, Washington, DC 20005 USA

Design and layout by Beth Elzer, AAAS Publication Services
See inside back cover for ordering information

Library of Congress Cataloging-in-Publication Data

Baker, Catherine, 1956-
    The evolution dialogues : science, Christianity, and the quest for
    understanding / by Catherine Baker ; James B. Miller, editor.
        p. cm.
        Includes bibliographical references and index.
        ISBN 0-87168-709-7
        1. Evolution (Biology)--Religious aspects--Christianity.
    2. Evolution (Biology) 3. Religion and science. I. Miller,
    James B. (James Bradley), 1942- II. Title.

BL263.B25 2006
231.7'652--dc22   2006042945

Table of Contents

Preface and Acknowledgements 5

Prologue 9

Chapter 1:
Science in Darwin's time

Dialogue 17

A period of unprecedented
scientific discovery 20

Finding evidence of extinction 21

Rethinking the age of the Earth 23

Pondering the succession of life 25

Darwin makes his contribution 28

Chapter 2:
Christianity in Darwin's time

Dialogue 35

The seamless blending of all knowledge . . . 38

The world as inferred from the Bible 39

Natural philosophy and natural theology 41

An evolving sense of history 44

Darwin's religious views 47

Chapter 3:
The theory of evolution

Dialogue 49

Evolution in action 52

Natural selection 54

Other evolutionary mechanisms 57

Microevolution and macroevolution 59

Evidence for evolution 62

Focus of current research 67

Chapter 4:
Initial responses to Darwin's theory

Dialogue 71

A topic of personal interest 74

Rejection 75

Qualified acceptance 77

Enthusiastic support 78

Evolution of scientific and public opinion . . . 81

Evolving Christian responses 84

The response from other religions 86

Buildup toward a backlash 87

Evolution on trial 90

Chapter 5:
The science behind evolution

Dialogue 93
What science is 97
Levels of scientific knowledge 100
The construction of knowledge
    about evolution 102
Certainty and uncertainty 103
Non-scientific interpretations of science . . . 105
What science is not 107

Chapter 6:
Christian worldviews

Dialogue 111
Defining Christianity 114
Foundations of Christianity 115
The Christian story 118
Christian belief and history 118
Contexts of knowing 121
Defining religion 122
Faith as the starting point 123
Contested knowledge 124

Chapter 7:
The world as explained by evolution

Dialogue 127
Diversity beyond measure 131
One big family 133
Life's origins 136
The arrival of plants and animals 138
Human origins 141
The future of evolution 145

Chapter 8:
Contemporary stances toward evolution

Dialogue 149
A touchy subject 153
"Scientific" creationism 156
"Intelligent design" 158
Scientists respond 164
Creation and evolution as complementary . . 168
Creation and evolution as interactive 170

Epilogue: Advancing beyond dialogue 173

Endnotes 181

Glossary 183

Appendix: Deep evolutionary time 199

Index 203

PREFACE AND ACKNOWLEDGEMENTS

The resource you are about to engage is an outcome of a series of consultations organized by the Program of Dialogue on Science, Ethics, and Religion (DoSER) of the American Association for the Advancement of Science (AAAS) from 2000 through 2003. These consultations brought together representatives of the scientific and Christian religious communities to explore what unique and constructive contribution a scientific society like the AAAS might make toward helping to resolve the public controversy centered on the teaching of evolution in the nation's public schools. It was recognized that given the history of the controversy, and the religious demographics of American society, it would be most appropriate to work in particular with Christian communities. A strong consensus emerged from these consultations that the most high-impact effort that AAAS could facilitate would be the production of a readily accessible educational resource on evolutionary science that could be used in the informal education programs of Christian religious communities. It was urged that the tone of the scientific presentation be modest and that the resource invite a positive religious engagement with evolutionary science. These initial consultations were made possible through support from the Esther A. and Joseph Klingenstein Fund.

Drawing from the participants in the consultations, the AAAS Dialogue program formed an editorial advisory committee to assist with the initial drafting of the resource. The members of the committee were: the Rev. Dan Dick (research manager, General Board of Discipleship of the United Methodist Church), Rev. Betty Holley (pastor of the Holy Trinity AME Church, high school math teacher at Xenia High School, and instructor in theology and ecology at Payne Theological Seminary), Rev. Dr. Judy Kohatsu (pastor of the Federated Church of Sandwich NH – United Methodist and American Baptist, material scientist), Dr. Wes McCoy (chair of the Department of Science, North Cobb High School, Kennesaw, GA), Dr. Alan Padgett (Professor of Systematic Theology at Luther Seminary), Dr. Robert J. Schneider (member of the Committee on Science, Technology and Faith of the Executive Council of the Episcopal Church in America), Dr. Sara Via (professor in the Departments of Biology and Entomology, University of Maryland), and Dr. Roger Willer (Associate for Studies on Church in Society, Evangelical Lutheran Church in America). Working with professional plain language writer, Catherine Baker, the advisory committee developed a basic outline for the resource as well as assisted in the determination of format including the use of a framing narrative. The preparation of the manuscript for the resource, its review, and field-testing were supported by the John Templeton Foundation as well as the Klingenstein Fund.

The editorial advisory committee reviewed the first drafts of each chapter and made substantive suggestions that were incorporated in later drafts. When these initial revisions of the resource were complete, the full text was submitted to a distinguished group of external reviewers with expertise in the evolutionary sciences, the history of science, science education, Christian theology, science and religion, and public policy. These reviewers included Margaret Kidwell (evolutionary biologist, University of Arizona), Ken Miller (cell biologist, Brown University), Richard Potts (paleoanthropologist, National Museum of Natural History – Smithsonian), Rodger Bybee (science educator and director, Biological Sciences Curriculum Study), Susan Musante (science educator, American Institute of Biological Sciences), John Staver (science educator, Kansas State University), Ronald Numbers (historian of science, University of Wisconsin), John Haught (Christian theologian, Georgetown University), Nancy Howell (Christian theologian, St. Paul School of Theology), Antje Jackelén (Christian theologian and director, Zygon Center for Religion and Science), Randall Isaacs, (physicist and director, American Scientific Affiliation), Michael Hill (educator, National Association of State Boards of Education), Eugenie Scott (anthropologist and director, National Center for Science Education), and Alexandra de Sousa (anthropologist, George Washington University).

A final set of edits was made based on feedback from groups representing the constituencies for which this resource was prepared. The work of carrying out this feedback process and collating the results was aided substantially by the efforts of Peyton West (evolutionary ecologist and senior program associate in the AAAS Program of Dialogue on Science, Ethics, and Religion).

While it may seem unusual for a resource produced by a scientific association to include a significant amount of material about religion, AAAS has from its inception been interested in the broad cultural significance of scientific and technological development, including the relationship of science and religion. Given the religious dimensions of the current and ongoing controversy about teaching evolution in the public schools, a resource that seeks to make a constructive contribution to resolving the issue will benefit from addressing these dimensions. As such, *The Evolution Dialogues* provides a mainstream descriptive account of the essentially Christian environment around, and response to, Darwin's *The Origin of Species.* The resource includes the general features of the Christian religious tradition in terms of its history and approach to understanding, and contemporary approaches to evolution that can found in Christian religious communities.

Finally, this resource would not have been possible without the encouragement and support of AAAS senior management, especially Alan Leshner (AAAS Executive Officer), Al Teich (AAAS Science and Policy Programs), and Shirley Malcom (AAAS Education and Human Resources). It is particularly indebted to the leadership of Connie Bertka (director, AAAS Program of Dialogue on Science, Ethics, and Religion) and her predecessor Audrey Chapman.

James B. Miller
Editor

Prologue

Angela Rawlett looked down at the limp little shark lying on a bed of newspapers and releasing the slight odor of formaldehyde. This was not the first time during vertebrate anatomy lab that the college freshman was thankful she had grown up on a farm. She had seen her share of gutted animals and had no hesitation dissecting worms or frogs. Nonetheless, she paused in wonder before this shark. There were no sharks in the Midwest. She'd never seen the ocean, much less a shark live or dead.

Her reverie was interrupted by the snort of her lab partner, Lenny.

"*Squalus acanthias*. Spiny dogfish. This guy is such a runt," he said. "I wish we could dissect a megalodon."

"What's a megalodon?" asked Angela. After six weeks of Lenny as a lab partner, she was used to his frequent displays of superficial knowledge.

"*Carcharadon megalodon*. Biggest shark that ever was," Lenny

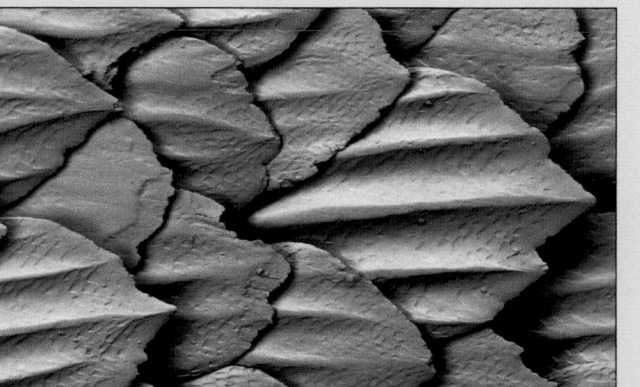

Placoid scales.

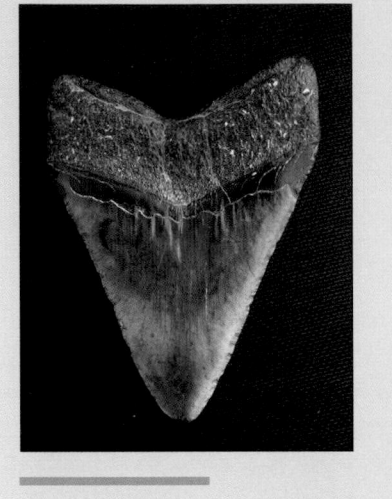

Carcharodon megalodon tooth.

answered. "Big as a Greyhound bus! Only it died out more than a million years ago."

Lenny's discourse on megalodon was interrupted by the lab instructor's voice. "Examine the skin of your specimen by running your fingers along its back gently, from posterior to anterior," he said. Angela put her hand on the shark's head.

"You're going the wrong way, Rawlett," said Lenny. "Start at the rump."

"The roughness you feel is the placoid scales, also known as the dermal denticles or skin-teeth," said the instructor. "If you look up here on my screen, you can see an enlarged image of these scales. Notice the similarity of shape with the shark's teeth, which evolved from these denticles."

Lenny pointed his pencil at the shark's mouth. "Megalodon was much more impressive. He was known as the giant-toothed shark, you know."

Over Lenny's voice, Angela could hear the instructor continuing to speak. "Take your scalpel now and remove a small piece of skin," he said. "Then examine this sample with your lens."

The talkative Lenny suddenly became deferential. "You first," he said. As in previous dissections, Lenny preferred to give the running commentary and let Angela do the actual work. She picked up the knife and neatly sliced a square of skin. Lenny studied it under the lens. "Rough as 40-grit sandpaper," he said. "You know people do use shark skin as sandpaper. Say, why don't you cut out a piece of your skin for comparison, Rawlett?"

"My turn, city boy," Angela retorted as she grabbed the lens from her lab partner. As she leaned over to study the specimen of skin, her necklace pendant dangled down from her neck.

"Hey, what's that?" said Lenny. He poked at the cross and grinned. Angela shoved him away and tucked the necklace back into her shirt. Then she stared back through the lens. But as she did so, she could hear him teasing her.

"You're one of those capital 'C' Christians, huh?" he said, smirking. "You believe all that stuff about the

The Evolution Dialogues

Garden of Eden and the six days of creation? I'll bet you think mega-lodon was washed away in Noah's Flood instead of going extinct."

Angela put down the lens, picked up the scalpel, flipped over the shark, and sliced it open between the pelvic and pectoral fins. That shut up Lenny. But after class, Angela could not get his comments out of her mind. There was a familiar ring to them, she realized. Her father gives her grief like that, but of a different sort.

During a recent visit home, Angela had happened to repeat some information that, ironically enough, she had picked up from Lenny. She had mentioned that the cow is a close relative of the whale, because whales are in a line of descent from a hoofed mammal that reentered the sea. "What nonsense you speak!" her father had replied. "Honestly, Angela, I don't know why you would believe that. We know where the whale came from. God put it there, in the water. It's written down for us, in Genesis. Is that college turning you away from God's word?"

Angela felt as though she were being pulled in two directions. "I love God and I think science is really neat," she thought to herself. "The creation story is meaningful to me, but what I've heard about evolution makes sense, too. Why do people expect me to take sides?"

Whales descend from a line of hoofed land mammals that returned to the sea.

PROLOGUE

The personal dilemma of Angela Rawlett, the main character of the story that threads through the chapters of *The Evolution Dialogues,* is not a unique one. Many university faculty report that students from traditional Christian backgrounds will approach them at the beginning of entry-level biology courses to confess their anxiety. What has the students worried is the conflict they anticipate between what they will be taught about evolution and what they already believe through their religious faith. This concern is not exclusive to college students. More and more teachers at the high school and middle school levels are also hearing about the misgivings students have when it comes time to study evolution.

A considerable number of parents, too, as well as school board members, teachers, school administrators, and community leaders, carry ambivalent or even hostile feelings about the teaching of evolutionary science. Many have acted on these concerns to propose, consider, and in some cases enact changes in their community's formal science education standards or curriculum models. The intent of such changes is to undermine or remove the teaching of evolution from the public education system.

But why? What accounts for the assumption held by a vocal minority of the Christian population that evolutionary theory is a threat to their religious beliefs? Historically, the dynamic between science and traditional religion has *not* been as conflict-filled as the general public has presumed. We know this from the work of a number of scholars of the past half century who have revisited this history. Many scientists and science teachers have been and are Christians. Many denominations of Christianity and many millions of Christians do not have trouble reconciling evolutionary biology with their religious traditions. Furthermore, evolutionary theory is one of the most substantiated theories in all of science, with an overwhelming wealth of data from various branches of study supporting it. So why has evolution been such a cultural flash point?

One answer to that question is that there are deep misunderstandings about what biological evolution is, what science itself is, and what views people of faith, especially Christians, have applied to their interpretations of the science. With this volume, AAAS seeks to correct some of those misunderstandings.

In this resource, we provide a brief yet thorough description of the origin, development, and contemporary state of evolutionary theory, of the science that produces it, and of the history of nature that results from the application of modern evolutionary theory. Parallel to that, we present an account of the cultural context in which the original theory appeared, the range of initial Christian reactions, how Christians have traditionally understood religious (as contrasted with scientific) knowledge, and alternative ways that Christians today respond to evolutionary theory.

Obviously, Christians are an intended audience for this volume, and we have developed it specifically with the intention of it being usable as part of Christian adult education programs. However, *The Evolution Dialogues* also has value in other educational settings: freshman biology courses, history of science classes, library resource collections, seminars, and education programs sponsored by religious groups other than Christian, to name a prospective few.

We also expect that some individual readers and groups of readers will vary in their focus and in the amount of time they have to read this material. The four odd-numbered chapters can be used together as a concise introduction to the nature of science and evolutionary theory. In parallel fashion, the four even-numbered chapters can be used as an introduction to the history of Christian interaction with evolutionary theory. The chapters also work in pairs thematically. So, for example, Chapters 1 and 2 both focus on 18th and 19th century developments, while Chapters 7 and 8 address contemporary understandings. In some cases, a single chapter might be most useful, such as Chapter 5 for readers looking for clarity on what science is and what it is not, or Chapter 8 for use with readers who have previously assumed that there is only one possible stance a Christian can take toward evolutionary theory. In some settings, the best way to use this resource might be to present the interweaving stories for discussion and reserve the chapters themselves for background reading.

Several additional elements are included in this teaching resource. A glossary is included at the end of the volume, and glossary words are highlighted in blue throughout the text. We have also appended metaphors for evolutionary time. Additional resources are listed to encourage readers to continue in their exploration of the issues surrounding the nexus of evolutionary theory and Christianity.

Not incidentally, our intent is to foster dialogue, which is why *The Evolution Dialogues* includes the storyline about Angela Rawlett. Much like the real-life college students of which she is a prototype, Angela is on a journey of discovery. She is not alone on this journey because she maintains connection with her family, church, and friends. Plus, she finds two mentors at her college: Dr. Laurel Dunbar, a scientist and her faculty advisor, and Rev. Dr. Phil Compton, a member of the campus ministry. Angela ventures into dialogue with these two mentors and as a result her understandings of science and faith are both enriched. Angela's story reflects how each of us comes to understand our world in community with others. It is a model for how individuals might use dialogue to find an accord between science and religion.

Other levels of dialogue besides the interpersonal are captured in this publication. There is the historical dialogue between Christians of today and their predecessors, and between scientists of today and their predecessors. There is the dialogue across communities, between Christians and scientists. Yet another set of dialogues is inferred: the ones going on today in the real world, before school boards and legislatures, in classrooms, in scientific laboratories, and in houses of religion. The emergence of wise and healthy decisions and perspectives from these settings depends in large degree on informed and open dialogue.

Some readers may think it odd that a scientific association such as AAAS has produced a publication that gives explicit attention to a particular religious tradition, Christianity, and that has as a primary target the members of that tradition. The emphasis on the American response also may seem strange given that evolutionary theory belongs to science, which is an international enterprise. Yet AAAS from its beginnings has recognized that the practice of science occurs in a broader cultural context, that the culture both affects and is affected by science, and that religious interests are a significant part of that cultural fabric.

While the public controversy surrounding evolutionary theory and its place in public science education are neither exclusively Christian nor American, the drama has been particularly intense within the Christian community in the United States, almost from the first moment Darwin published his theory in 1859.

Surveys indicate that more than 75 percent of adult Americans today identify themselves with one or another branch of Christianity. Demographically, those most troubled by evolution and most active in challenging it as part of the public school curriculum are identified with Christianity. So, at the very least, a resource that seeks to overcome deep misunderstandings in the American public about evolutionary theory, science, and cultural responses to both must give attention to Christianity as practiced in this country.

In the modern era, the scriptural literalism of American-born fundamentalist Christianity has influenced a small minority of believers from other faiths. In a departure from their respective traditions, such believers have begun to read their sacred scriptures more literally, and this has challenged their attitudes toward modern science. Nonetheless, non-Christians who oppose evolutionary theory have not been the activists in the realm of public policy. The responses to evolutionary theory from three other prominent faiths — Judaism, Islam, and Buddhism — are addressed briefly and for comparative purposes in Chapter 4.

Those branches of the Christian family tree that have found a way to accommodate or integrate evolution into their belief systems have tended to be less publicly engaged, because they have seen less at stake. This volume is one effort by AAAS to help engage that latter group, because very much *is* at stake. We are talking about the quality of public science education and the scientists who come out of that enterprise, the integrity of science as an independent enterprise, and the constitutional division between church and state. For people who value such things, *The Evolution Dialogues* can be part of their education and a lever that lifts them into greater involvement in today's public dialogue.

Science in Darwin's time

Angela Rawlett knocked on the door of her advisor's office and was greeted by the sight of Dr. Laurel Dunbar half-hidden beneath a desk laden with papers and small potted plants.

"Ah, hello Angela," said the biology professor as she crawled out from under the desk. "Please excuse me. I was hooking up my new flat screen so I can finally junk this old monitor." She stood up clutching a pair of cables and, with her foot, pulled forward a chair for the student.

"I hadn't forgotten our appointment," Dr. Dunbar said brightly. "You're here to discuss your schedule for next semester, am I right?" The young woman nodded her head. The professor moved the cables to her right hand and with her left pulled a course schedule out from the jumble on her desk. From her standing position, she leaned over her desk and began flipping through the pages. "Let's start with the courses in your major," she said. "Obviously, since you're taking Bio 121 this fall, you'll be following that up with 122 in the spring."

Angela removed a stack of books from the offered chair and sat down. "Umm, actually, I was thinking of jumping ahead and taking Plant Biology, Bio 224."

Dr. Dunbar paused to glance over at her student. "In that case, you would be in my class. So I'm flattered. But it doesn't really make sense. Why skip over a course required for your major? It's a prerequisite, in fact, for the plant biology course."

Angela pointed to the description of Bio 122 in the catalog. "See here, it's called 'Evolution, Ecology, and Diversity.' I just don't think that would be interesting."

The professor let out a hoot of laughter. "Not interesting? That's like saying life isn't interesting. It's *fascinating*." She waved her arms and the cables in her hand flew about like live snakes. Angela shrunk back.

"Oh, sorry," said the professor, setting the cables down on top of her desk chair. "So what's your real reason?"

"I'm just not sure I want to study all that."

Dr. Dunbar took a look at Angela, who was tilting her head down. Her eyes were hidden under her hair. "Hey, what's the problem here?" asked the professor in a kindly way.

Angela looked up. "I just think I might not be comfortable in that class."

The advisor sat down in her chair so that she was eye level with the student. "Go on," she said.

Angela watched Dr. Dunbar squirm in her chair to extract the cables beneath her, and then spoke. "We didn't study evolution at my high school, and I really don't know that much about it," she said. "Except that my dad thinks it's wrong. He says it would mean that our ancestors are monkeys."

"And you don't think that's interesting?" asked Dr. Dunbar with a wink. "Actually, Angela," she continued, "your father is half correct. Evolution does suggest that far back in time, an ancestor of ours *and* of modern monkeys was a furry, tree-loving primate of some sort. But that's not such an awful thing, when you come to understand it."

Angela pondered a minute. "It's not just the topic that's the problem. I don't think I'd fit in."

"Fit in? You mean with the other students in the class?"

"I've been teased a bit already. My lab partner seems to think I'm backward because I go to church."

"Been poking fun at you, huh?" The professor looked at the course schedule. "Can you fit this Bio 122 class into your schedule? It's with Otis Brown. This class will fill up even though it's at 8 a.m. Otis knows how to communicate science, and he's — he'll make you feel comfortable."

Angela hesitated.

The fossil of a hominid mandible (lower jaw bone) determined by radiometric dating to be about 4.5 million years old.

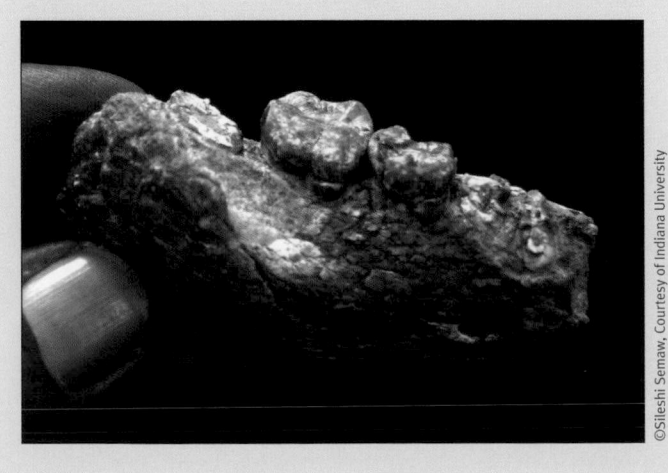

©Sileshi Semaw, Courtesy of Indiana University

The Evolution Dialogues

The professor stood up and began digging through her desk. "Look here. I think I can convince you that evolution is more interesting than it is frightening. Here's an article about evolution in strains of the AIDS virus." She picked up a sheath of papers, then set it down again. "Maybe not. That prose is a little dense." Shuffling through another pile, the professor pulled out a science magazine. "How about this? It's an article about the find of hobbit-sized skeletons on an Indonesian island. Talk about interesting! Now somewhere around here I also have a wonderful thesis paper by my grad student describing adaptations of carnivorous plant species to...."

The Venus fly-trap, *Dionaea muscipula*, is one of 595 species of carnivorous plants.

She turned around and looked at Angela, who still wore a doubtful expression on her face.

"If I can't appeal to your emotions, I'll try reason," said Dr. Dunbar. "Remember what Dobzhanksy said."

"Dob ... who?" asked the student.

"A great geneticist, Theodosius Dobzhasky — and a Russian Orthodox Christian, I might add. He said and I quote, 'Nothing in biology makes sense except in the light of evolution.' You need this foundation if you really want to understand plants."

"Actually, it's not plants I'm so interested in, it's animals," Angela asserted. "I'd like to be a veterinarian."

"The same applies. Evolution helps us make sense of animals, of plants, of humans, of the Earth, even of the universe." Dr. Dunbar paused, then looked hard at Angela. "What can I say to convince you?"

Angela looked back sheepishly.

"You remember, don't you," said the professor, "that science is based on the study of evidence?"

"Yes, of course" said Angela. "I think I know where you're heading."

"And where's that?" asked the professor.

"You think that before I judge evolution, I should check it out for myself."

Dr. Dunbar clapped her hands together. "So what do you think?"

"I think I'll think about it," said Angela as she threw her palms up in mock surrender. "Give me that article about the hobbit people."

CHAPTER 1

Science in Darwin's time

Mary Anning with her faithful dog Tray standing on the foreshore of her home town Lyme Regis, Dorset, with the famous outcrop "Golden Cap" in the background.

©The Natural History Museum, London

A period of unprecedented scientific discovery

Mary Anning (1799–1847) was an unlikely figure to become one of the greatest fossil-finders of all time. An unschooled girl, Mary was born in Lyme Regis, on the southern coast of England, to a cabinetmaker who died when she was still a child. To support themselves, Mary and her mother and brother collected from the incredible fossil-rich cliffs near their home and sold pieces of old bone and shell as souvenirs to visitors of the seaside town. They also marketed the more valuable specimens to museums and private collectors. As an adult, Mary became expert at excavating, mounting, and documenting fossils. Among her many significant finds, she discovered the very first specimen of plesiosaurus, a large and flippered marine reptile.

This was at a time when many people in the western world were caught up in the spirit of scientific discovery. In the early 19th century, the label "scientist" had not yet entered the common vocabulary, and the academic criteria by which a scientist is defined today were not in place. Many scholars, clerics, members of the affluent classes, and common citizens pursued natural history, as the study and classification of nature was then called.

In Russia, across Europe, and overseas in North America, all sorts of people were digging fossils out of the ground — not only from seashores like that of Lyme Regis, but also from mine shafts, tunnels, excavations,

The Evolution Dialogues

caves, quarries, and old lakebeds. Their discoveries of strange bones raised questions about where the species they had once belonged to might be or have gone. Ship captains, traders, and ordinary sailors were returning from expeditions around the globe with plant and animal specimens that collectively revealed an astonishing and previously unrecognized diversity to life. Professional land surveyors and "gentlemen geologists" were studying the patterns in the layers of rock that form the ground and trying to decipher what they indicated about the forces that had shaped the Earth. Through these and other pursuits, people were seeking to discover the natural causes used by God to create and manage the world.

The Ammonite is perhaps the most widely known fossil. These sea creatures lived between 415 to 65 million years ago and became extinct with the dinosaurs.

Finding evidence of extinction

Georges Cuvier (1769–1832) was among those who were trying to make sense of all the new discoveries. He was a zoologist, interested in the structure, functions, and classifications of animals, and he was one of the first persons ever to study fossil evidence as a means of learning about prehistoric time. Through his position at the Museum of Natural History in Paris, Cuvier was able to closely examine its huge collection of preserved animals and fossil remains. He made an important contribution to the discipline of science through his painstaking focus on empirical evidence — on observable facts rather than speculation.

Cuvier built on the work of Carl Linnaeus (1707–1778) and Georges-Louis Leclerc, Comte de Buffon (1707–1788), two eminent anatomists of the previous generation, to propose a new classification system for organisms. According to Cuvier, living types could be sorted into four basic groups based on body type: vertebrates (having a backbone), mollusks (having a

Cuvier's four basic body types were vertebrates, mollusks, articulates, and radiates.

shell), articulates (for example, insects and segmented worms), and radiates (symmetrical creatures such as starfish). Cuvier's original taxonomy has been much revised since, but it was important as a new, nonlinear way to consider the relationship of species to each other. As such, it helped overturn a once-dominant doctrine called the "great chain of being." According to that doctrine, the origins of which dated back to ancient Greece, all living things fall into a single hierarchy that ascends from the most simple up to the most complex, with human beings at the pinnacle of this straight line.

The assumption that went along with the old hierarchical ordering of life is that each species in the chain has its own ideal structure and function. Each species has always existed on Earth in its perfectly suited form, and each would exist in such form eternally. Cuvier helped overturn these ideas. Comparing the skeletons of elephants of India and Africa to each other and to the fossilized remains of mammoths that had been discovered in Siberia, Europe, and North America, Cuvier declared that each belonged to a distinct species. Furthermore, he noted, no living mammoth had ever been found. He published these findings in 1796. After conducting several more anatomical comparisons of living mammals to similar-seeming fossils, he eventually concluded that virtually all fossils represented extinct lines. These extinctions broke the great chain.

To account for such disappearance, Cuvier speculated that some great series of natural disasters, which he called "revolutions," had occurred. Each disaster, often involving flooding, wiped out many or perhaps most inhabitants, but their remains were preserved in the sediment that collected beneath the waters. In some unknown way, a new set of creatures replaced the old. Because no human fossils were known in Cuvier's time, he concluded that human beings had only come into existence since the last revolution.

The Evolution Dialogues

Rethinking the age of the Earth

Before the 19th century, it was popularly assumed that the Earth had been created just a few thousand years before. A widely held belief that the world was created in 4,004 B.C. was based in large part on the record of events and lineages recorded by the Bible. But in 1778, Comte de Buffon proposed that the planet was actually around 75,000 years old. Buffon arrived at his figure for the Earth's age based on experiments heating and cooling iron balls and other materials. He extrapolated from these test results to estimate the length of time it would take to cool the molten mass of the Earth that, he conjectured, had been created along with the solar system's other planets when a comet crashed into the sun.

This estimate of an old Earth was soon displaced by an even more radical number. A physician, industrial chemist, and geologist from Scotland named James Hutton (1726–1797) claimed that the Earth had to be immensely old — millions of years old. Hutton first made this assertion at a scientific lecture in 1785 that convinced no one. As a biographer of Hutton has written, his proposition was unbelievable: "It would be akin to being told today that the sun is not really the source of the Earth's heat and light, or that there actually is complex life on the moon."[1]

Hutton had no proof for his claim of the Earth's age — that would come later, with chemical methods for isotopic dating of rocks. However, from what he could see on his farm and the surrounding territory, Hutton knew that natural processes operate slowly. For this reason, he inferred that it must have taken millions of years for the Earth to acquire its weathered mountains, jutting outcrops of rock, valley depressions, and other features. Indeed, Hutton argued, the Earth's history was indefinite in time: a cycle of gradual destruction and renewal so vast that the geological record left "no vestige of a beginning … No prospect of an end."

Hutton put his ideas together in a book, *The Theory of the Earth,* published in 1795, in which the above quotation appeared. But he wrote in difficult prose and his ideas remained obscure until well after the turn of the century. Then Hutton's ideas were championed by an Englishman, Charles Lyell (1797–1875). A gentleman farmer and lawyer, Lyell keenly pursued an interest in the natural world, and for his many contributions to the study of the Earth, he is known as "the founder of modern geology."

Lyell made careful observations of cliffs and other rock walls. Such vertical surfaces gave evidence of **strata** (layers) of **sedimentary rock** preserved above strata of **igneous rock**. Sedimentary rock is formed from particles of older rock, shell, decomposed organisms, and salt that have

Nicolaus Steno, a 17th century Roman Catholic priest,
was the first to propose
that rock strata were
formed horizontally when
particles of earth settled to
the bottom of a body of
water and that the lower
strata were formed earlier
than the higher.

been compressed together under a body of water, while igneous rock is made from crystals and formed at very high temperatures from molten material. In some locations, the two layers of rock would be upended and eroded. Sometimes a rock wall would display shafts of igneous rock piercing through strata of sedimentary rock.

Lyell sought to account for the strange patterns in the rock strata and the endless variety of rock formations on the Earth's surface. He eventually developed an explanatory theory that later came to be called **uniformitarianism** for its reliance on uniform or usual (as opposed to catastrophic) causes to explain geological change. The title of Lyell's widely read work, first published in 1830, sums it up quite neatly — *Principles of Geology: An Attempt to Explain the Former Changes of the Earth's Surface by Reference to Causes now in Operation.*

According to this theory, the appearance of the Earth has resulted from the incessant actions of nature: wind, rain, freezing, thawing, earthquakes, volcanoes, and storms. Natural phenomena that humans could observe — such as the washing away of a field's soil in a rainstorm, a landslide suddenly descending from a cliff, or the wearing away of a shoreline over the years by the beating tide — were the same forces that had shaped the Earth all throughout its long history.

More specifically, the process worked like this: weathering and erosion would wear away the topmost layer of the Earth's crust, which would then be washed away by stream and river into the ocean bottom. Over time these particles would accumulate and form new layers of sedimentary rock, at the same time capturing and preserving the bones and shells of creatures that had died, creating fossils. Heat within the Earth from its molten core would lift layers of the ocean floor forcefully upward, creating new land.

There was no room in this view for extraordinary, worldwide catastrophes such as a flood that in one fell swoop changed the entire face of the Earth. Rather, natural laws operating over great expanses of time created small, steady, and relatively gradual change. The most significant difference between Hutton's and Lyell's thinking was that the latter argued that change was not cyclical; rather, it was directionless.

Pondering the succession of life

New ideas about how change might have occurred *to* the Earth were paralleled by new thoughts on how change might have occurred to life *on* the Earth. One of the curiosities that emerged from studies of the geological strata was that each layer appeared to contain different assortments of plant and animal fossils. Ascending toward the surface, layers tended to contain more complex organisms. For example, lower strata contained only fossils of shells, fossilized wood, and coral. Higher strata also contained fossils of plants, fish, amphibians, and reptiles, followed by birds and mammals. This evidence was what had led Cuvier to conclude that natural revolutions had wiped out certain life forms, which were then somehow replaced, and that humans had arrived after the last upheaval. Cuvier suggested that perhaps each new population either migrated into the empty territory or was created in some new, spontaneous occurrence — based on what was known, he could not say. Because in Cuvier's time there was little evidence in the fossil record of small gradual changes within and between species, he concluded that **organic succession** (a phrase referring to evolution) was impossible.

But Cuvier's predecessor Buffon — who had proposed the theory of a 75,000-year-old-Earth — believed that a kind of organic succession did occur. Buffon asserted that the world's great variety of species developed through degeneration from a smaller number of ideal types. For example, lions, tigers,

Tigers, according to Buffon, are a degenerate form of an ideal feline type.

The Temple of Nature

By Erasmus Darwin

CANTO I
PRODUCTION OF LIFE

"ORGANIC LIFE beneath the shoreless waves
Was born and nurs'd in Ocean's pearly caves;
First forms minute, unseen by spheric glass,
Move on the mud, or pierce the watery mass;
These, as successive generations bloom
New powers acquire, and larger limbs assume;
Whence countless groups of vegetation spring,
And breathing realms of fin, and feet, and wing.

"Thus the tall Oak, the giant of the wood,
Which bears Britannia's thunders on the flood;
The Whale, unmeasured monster of the main,
The lordly Lion, monarch of the plain,
The Eagle soaring in the realms of air,
Whose eye undazzled drinks the solar glare,
Imperious man, who rules the bestial crowd,
Of language, reason, and reflection proud,
With brow erect who scorns this earthly sod,
And styles himself the image of his God;
Arose from rudiments of form and sense,
An embryon point, or microscopic ens!

and domestic cats were all degenerated from some original feline animal. An "internal mold" prevented species from varying too much from the original, according to Buffon. As evidence for this idea, he pointed out that hybrid animals such as mules were sterile — they could not produce descendants. Thus for Buffon and many others, variety within types could evolve, but no evolution could occur from one type to another.

Buffon's degenerative depiction of evolution contrasted with several progressive scenarios, such as the one proposed by Erasmus Darwin (1731–1802), grandfather of Charles Darwin (1809–1882). A doctor by profession and a devoted student of nature, Erasmus Darwin was also a **freethinker**. In the early 19th century, this meant that though he believed in God, he did not believe in the authority of organized religion or in the infallibility of the Bible. This gave him the space to imagine that, over time, God had created a sequence of species, each a slight improvement on the previous one. Starting with a microscopic form, God had worked away through creation, up to the ultimate masterpiece — humankind.

All of life was connected, in Erasmus Darwin's view: "all warm-blooded animals have arisen from one living filament, which the great **First Cause** endued with animality, with the power of acquiring new parts, attended with new propensities, directed by irritations, sensations, volitions, and associations, and thus possessing the faculty of continuing to improve by its own inherent activity, and of delivering down these improvements by generation to its posterity, world without end!" Erasmus Darwin published this thought and related ideas in *Zoonomia, or, the Laws of Organic Life*, the first volume of which appeared in 1794. He also put these conjectures into poetry such as "The Temple of Nature," published in 1802.

At nearly the same time but quite independently, a French naturalist named Jean-Baptiste Lamarck (1744–1829) came up with a somewhat sim-

The Evolution Dialogues

ilar idea. In *Philosophie Zoologique* published in 1809, Lamarck speculated that there was a "nervous fluid" inborn into each creature that impelled it toward greater complexity. As an organism's needs changed in response to environmental changes such as colder climate, drought, or scarcity of food, it would change how it used its body. Parts would shrink or grow depending on how much they were used. In this way, an animal might grow a longer neck, acquire fur, or learn how to swim. Such changes, acquired during the lifetime rather than inborn, would be inherited by the next generation of that organism.

With Lamarck, there was no such thing as extinction. The less perfect change into the more perfect, in what he called **transmutation**. Lamarck used observations from nature to back up his theory. He pointed to the presence of nonfunctional structures in animals as an indicator of parts no longer used and to the fact that embryos have structures such as tails that do not always develop in the adult organism.

Herbert Spencer (1820–1903) was the first to apply the word "evolution" to natural history and also to nearly any historical process such as

Lamarck proposed that characteristics like the length neck or fur or the ability to swim could be acquired by the action of an animal during its lifetime and passed on to its offspring.

the evolution of the mind or the evolution of societies. This British intellectual, born in 1820, believed that such processes all share the tendency to grow in size, complexity, and differentiation. For example, living organisms evolve from single-celled creatures into much larger life forms that have complex bodies with specialized parts such as heart and lungs. In the same way, families and small communities progressively evolve into larger societies in which there is a greater degree of specialization of activity. Spencer developed his ideas about evolution in a series of publications that included the 1862 work *First Principles*. Spencer was a philosopher, not a biologist or a geologist. He could not propose any particular mechanism by which evolution would occur except to endorse a Lamarckian form of acquired characteristics, or so-called "use inheritance."

As an undergraduate, Darwin was more interested in the study of nature in the field than in his classroom studies.

Darwin makes his contribution

It was into this era that Charles Darwin was born — into a time of industrial change, social ferment, and scientific upheaval. It was a time when, based upon accumulating evidence, people were grappling with the possibility of a world that was not stable but had undergone a long history of remarkable change.

Born in 1809, Charles Darwin was the son of Robert Darwin (1766–1848), a doctor, and the grandson of Erasmus Darwin, also a doctor. Charles' father pushed him to follow in the family profession, and so Darwin studied medicine at the University of Edinburgh. He soon learned that he was not at all suited for medicine. However, he did enjoy his self-directed study of nature: taking long observational walks through the countryside; collecting plant, animal, and insect specimens; and examining life under the microscope. After two years, his father accepted the fact that Charles could not abide medicine and so advised him to study for the clergy. Darwin moved to Cambridge University, where again he was less interested in his required theological subjects than in his studies of nature, which he conducted under the guidance of some talented mentors.

At that time, a few fortunate men with interests like Darwin's could hire themselves out to be the resident naturalists on sailing ships. Darwin avidly sought such a post. In 1831, upon receiving his bachelor's degree and when he was 23, he convinced his father to let him serve aboard the H.M.S. Beagle as a companion to the ship's captain, Robert FitzRoy (1805–1865). This particular ship had a commission to test new clocks for the British Navy and to map the coastline of South America, and it was embarking on a five-year, round-the-world journey. Darwin did not have the official title of ship's naturalist but he served in that capacity.

In December, the Beagle set off for points in South America, New Zealand, and Australia, stopping off at various islands en route. At each landing, while the captain and crew did their mapping, Darwin carefully studied the local terrain and collected specimens. He explored the Brazilian jungle, dug up fossil mammals in Argentina, climbed the Andes Mountains, witnessed an exploding volcano, lived through an earthquake, and explored coral reefs in the Pacific. But the most important experience of the whole trip was his visit to the Galapagos. Off the west coast of South America, this cluster of volcanic islands was home to a remarkable population of birds and tortoises and other animals. Of great interest to Darwin was the fact that the occupants of each island varied slightly from their neighbors. For example, each island had many birds, but each island's birds were slightly different. Darwin later learned, after having specimens studied by anatomy expert Richard Owen (1804–1865) back in London, that the birds on each island were all from the same family of songbird, the finch.

On his trip, Darwin had brought along the first volume of Lyell's *Principles of Geology.* This was the work in which Lyell persuasively argued that the Earth's surface was shaped by natural forces effecting small changes over great spans of time. Darwin's careful study of geological formations as he sailed around the world convinced him that Lyell was correct. He began to think that, in likewise fashion, natural forces over time might have created the abundant variety of life that he was witnessing in his years-long journey.

But how? Darwin got his first sense of an answer after the voyage, when he read *An Essay on the Principle of Population* by the clergyman Thomas Malthus (1766–1834). In this book, published in 1798, Malthus noted that humans — and any other breeding form of life — create far more offspring than can survive off available resources. Starvation, plague, interspecies violence, and other forces keep populations in check.

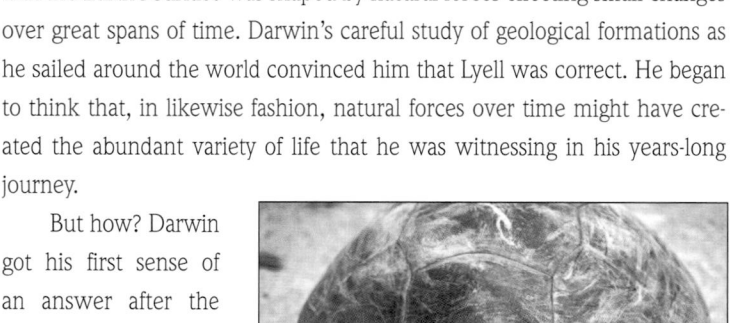

On the Galapagos Islands, Darwin encountered many distinctive species, such as the giant land tortoises, the frigate bird, and the marine iguana.

Reading this, Darwin had the insight that those individuals with traits more **adaptive** in their environment than others — for example, the ones that could more quickly elude predators, that were better at finding food, or that were better able to hide — would be the ones to survive the competition for resources long enough to produce offspring. Those individuals that did survive would pass on their more adaptive characteristics to their progeny, who again would have a better survival rate. Those with even slightly less adaptive traits would contribute fewer offspring. Eventually the most adaptive characteristics would come to dominate the species. As many such characteristics changed over time through a lineage of descendants, a new species would emerge. This is called **speciation**. The diversity of life reflects the fact that different traits are advantageous to survival in different environments.

The finches were a telling example. Darwin surmised that many generations ago, members of one original species had flown from the mainland of South America to the Galapagos. Their descendants had nested and bred on different islands, and over time, each island's residents acquired a unique assortment of characteristics most suited to their particular environment — for example, beak length and shape best adapted to the seeds their island provided. Eventually, the birds of each island diverged into separate species.

Darwin would come to call this "descent with modification." For a long time, he avoided the term "evolution" because it was commonly used in his time to describe the development of life, such as a seed growing into a tree or an embryo growing into an adult human.

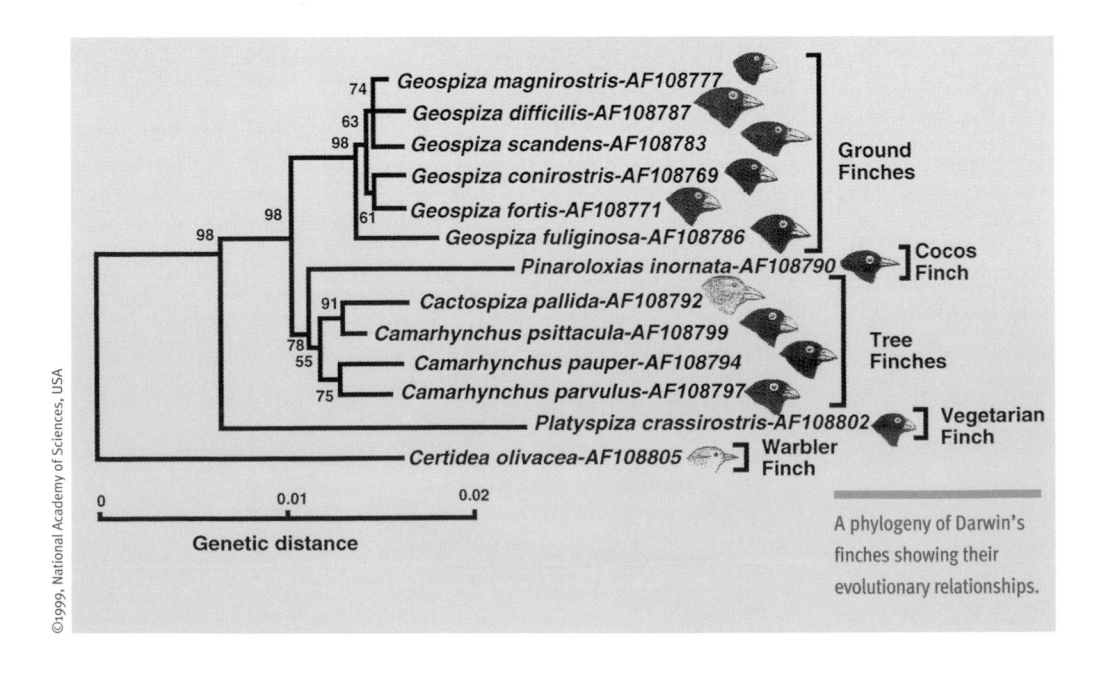

A phylogeny of Darwin's finches showing their evolutionary relationships.

The Evolution Dialogues

In Darwin's view, species change moved toward the more complex but not in any progressive or regressive direction. The changes that were preserved were merely the ones that best suited survival. **Natural selection** was the term he applied to the mechanism by which characteristics most adapted to the environment would pass on from one generation to the next. Later Darwin adopted a phrase coined by the philosopher Herbert Spencer: "survival of the fittest."

When he returned from the Beagle journey, Darwin was already known in scientific circles: a paper of his on the formation of coral reefs had been published while he was still at sea, and fossil mammals he had shipped ahead had generated some attention. With an allowance from his father, Darwin set himself up as an independent scholar. Over the next decades, he pursued a variety of scientific interests, but his main preoccupation was to develop his theory about evolution, meticulously build evidence in support of this theory, and draft a manuscript about it. He talked with farmers, pigeon fanciers, and dog breeders to learn how favored characteristics could be carried forward through generations of animals. He raised pigeons himself. He spent years comparing the anatomy of barnacle species. He studied other natural processes that would play into evolution, such as migration of

Darwin drew from his own experience as a pigeon breeder to infer how certain features can be selected by means of differential reproduction in nature.

birds, plant reproduction, and dispersal of seeds. He read prodigiously, and he corresponded extensively with other researchers.

But it was not until 1858 — 22 years after he had visited the Galapagos — that Darwin went public with his theory of evolution. The impetus was correspondence he received in 1858 from Alfred Russel Wallace (1823–1913), a naturalist who financed his explorations around the world by collecting and selling animal and insect specimens. Wallace had sent Darwin a handwritten essay with a note asking him to look it over. The essay sketched out ideas that were very similar to Darwin's about evolution, even using the expression "natural selection." Darwin realized that he was about to be preempted by another scientist because he had delayed so long in publishing. He turned to friends for advice, and his colleagues Charles Lyell and Joseph Hooker (1814–1879) arranged for a co-presentation of papers by both Darwin and Wallace at a scientific meeting in London.

Charles Darwin was 50 years old when *Origin of Species* was published. He had worked on his theory of descent with modification by means of natural selection for more than 20 years.

Following that meeting, in 1859, Darwin published *On the Origin of Species by Means of Natural Selection, or the Preservation of Favoured Races in the Struggle for Life*. This was a book-length condensation of the lengthy manuscript he had been drafting for years. It sold out immediately and has been in print ever since.

In *Origin of Species*, Darwin only touched upon human evolution. In a concluding paragraph, he said that with his theory, "light will be thrown on the origin of man and his history." He was well aware this would be the sticking point for those who believed that humans held a special position in God's creation. In his lifetime, Darwin published several more books developing more evidence for evolution, and in 1863, he tackled the sensitive subject of human evolution head on, in *The Descent of Man*.

As Darwin himself acknowledged, he did not invent the idea of evolution. However, he presented a tremendous amount of logical argument based on scientific evidence to support his conclusions of how evolution occurred. Most importantly, he gave evolution a mechanism: natural selection. This mechanism could be studied as a natural process, independent of supernatural and therefore untestable explanations. Later, the fields of

The Evolution Dialogues

genetics and molecular biology would supply the particular physical details of how characteristics varied and were transmitted from one generation to another.

In 1866, Gregor Mendel (1822–1884), an Augustinian monk, published the results of his extensive research on inheritance of traits in pea plants. When his paper was "discovered" independently by three researchers in 1900, the "laws of inheritance" that he described became the foundation for the development of the field of genetics. Some initially thought that Mendel's laws would be sufficient to account for biological variation and so would be a rival to Darwin's theory of evolution. However, it became clear that Mendelian genetics explains much of the pattern of variation that Darwin observed among offspring. It is on this variation that natural selection operates to bring about descent with modification.

The blending of evidence from the fields of evolutionary biology and genetics would, in the mid-20th century, come to be called the **modern synthesis**. Through the addition of research from many thousands of scientists in dozens of branches of study, the theory of evolution itself has been refined — has evolved, as it were — into the broad, overarching explanation of biological change and diversity that is overwhelmingly accepted by scientists today.

FURTHER READING

1. *The Abyss of Time: Unraveling the mystery of the Earth's age*, Claude C. Albritton, Jr. (Dover Publications, 2002)

2. *The Discovery of Time*, Stephen Toulmin and June Goodfield (University Of Chicago Press, 1982)

3. *Evolution: The remarkable history of a scientific theory*, Edward J. Larson (Modern Library, 2004)

4. *The Seashell on the Mountaintop: A story of science, sainthood, and the humble genius who discovered a new history of the Earth*, Alan Cutler (Dutton, 2003)

5. *Thinking about the Earth: A history of ideas in geology*, David Oldroyd (Harvard University Press, 1996)

Christianity in Darwin's Time

Angela Rawlett tentatively stepped inside the small brick building that housed the campus ministry offices. A tall man with rimless spectacles was leaning against a doorway in the reception room, reading a book. Angela noticed the title: *The Introvert's Guide to Conversation.*

"Hello," said the college freshman. "I have an appointment at 3:30 with Doctor Compton... or is it Reverend Compton?"

"Just call me Phil," the man answered. "I've been expecting you. Please come into my office."

Phil offered her some coffee, which she declined, and a comfortable upholstered chair, which she accepted. He sat down across from her in a second armchair and in a few minutes of conversation deftly extracted the details of her background. Then he glanced at an appointment card. "It says here that you wanted to talk about a possible switch in majors. I'm wondering how this is a religious concern for you. Have you talked to your academic advisor?"

"Yes, I did, sort of," said Angela. "But I wanted to make sure I'm doing the right thing. I used to talk about important decisions with people from my church back home, so I thought before I made this decision, I'd talk to somebody like that up here."

"Sensible," Phil said. "Tell me about your thinking."

"I thought I had to be a biology major to go on to vet school," explained Angela. "I've found out that's not true. So I was thinking I might major in something else."

"Are you taking a biology class now?"

"Yes," said Angela. "Vertebrate anatomy. I just dissected a shark last week."

"Not my cup of tea," said Phil, putting his coffee cup down. "But I sense from your tone of voice that you like it. Yet you say you don't want to continue in biology."

"Well I do but I don't. You see, I ..." Angela's voice drifted into silence. The minister was silent too. He looked at Angela and his soft brown eyes penetrated through the lenses of his glasses.

"The class I'm taking right now is fine," Angela said. "It's all about bones and tissues and homologies — you know, structural similarities. But next semester, I'm supposed to take Bio 122. 'Evolution, Ecology, and Diversity.' I would have to study evolution. So you see."

"I'm not sure I see. Evolution is a problem?"

"Well, *yeah*," said Angela. She looked up nervously at the campus minister but relaxed when he placidly drank from his coffee cup.

"That's good," Phil responded after a pause. "We know the problem. In fact, I have had other students come to me with similar concerns."

Angela raised her eyebrows. "Really? What did they say?"

Phil took another sip of coffee before he spoke. "Each student is unique, of course. But if I read you correctly, like those other students, you feel a tension between what you have been raised to believe about the creation of life on Earth and what you might learn in your evolution class."

Angela nodded her head. "I'm not saying I won't ever take Bio 122," she answered. "I'm just not sure I'm ready to take it yet."

"Certainly," said Phil, "but postponing that required course does 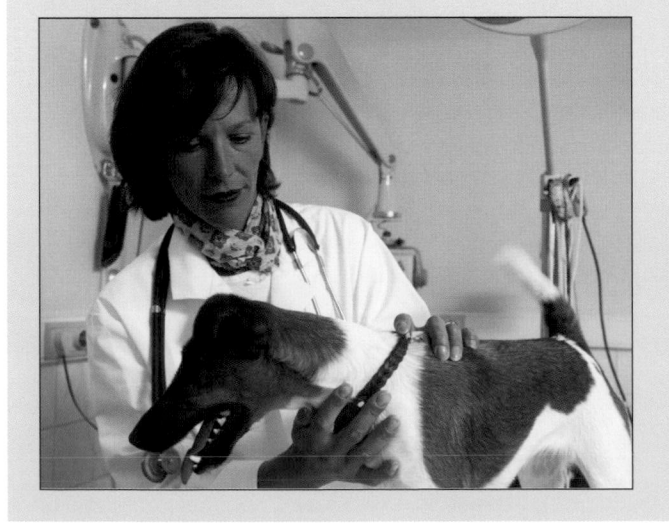 make a biology major more difficult." He leaned back into his chair, and looked straight at Angela. "So if not biology, what then? You'd better stay away from geology or anthropology. Evolution lurks there, too. You might be safe in English or Latin ... but by all means, avoid linguistics."

From the look on the minister's face, Angela detected that he thought he had said something amusing. "I wasn't thinking about any of those majors," she said. "I was thinking about accounting."

"Always useful," Phil responded. "But counting animals is not the same as learning about them." He picked up a book from the coffee table between them. "Let me make a point by way of example. Pick a Psalm, any Psalm," he muttered as he thumbed through the pages. "Here — are you familiar with Psalm 104?"

Of the half dozen psalms Angela had memorized, 104 was not among them.

"'O Lord, how manifold are your works!'" Phil recited softly. "'In wisdom you have made them all; the Earth is full of your creatures.' That's wonderful, isn't it? You agree that the Earth is full of God's creatures?"

"Yes," said Angela, cautiously.

"So how about this line from the same Psalm? 'You have set the Earth upon its foundations, so that it never shall move at any time.' You agree that the Earth never moves?"

"Of course not. But that's metaphorical."

"Maybe to us. Was it to the author of Psalm 104?" asked Phil. "As we see here, Angela, there are some readings of Scripture that are simply not consistent with our expanding knowledge of God's creation."

"Are you saying parts of the Bible are wrong?"

"Not at all. I'm saying that we are sometimes required by our growing awareness of God's manifold works to find deeper interpretations."

"So you think I should go ahead and stick with biology."

"My opinion is not relevant," said Phil mildly. "However, I will say that sometimes we deepen our Christian faith when we allow it to be challenged by our experiences in this very real world."

"A test," Angela responded. "You're daring me to take that evolution class."

"Only if you think you should."

"Let me see that Psalm," said Angela. She read aloud: "Yonder is the great and wide sea with its living things too many to number, creatures both small and great. There move the ships, and there is that Leviathan, which you have made for the sport of it.'" She paused, looking over at Phil. "Leviathan?"

"Sea monster. Possibly refers to a whale."

"Whale?" Angela uttered quietly. "I've been wondering about whales." She looked straight at her religious advisor. "Okay. I'll pray on it."

The Bible is the common literary foundation for all Christians. Throughout the history of Christianity the Bible has been interpreted and reinterpreted by numerous translators, church leaders and particular Christian communities.

CHAPTER 2

Christianity in Darwin's time

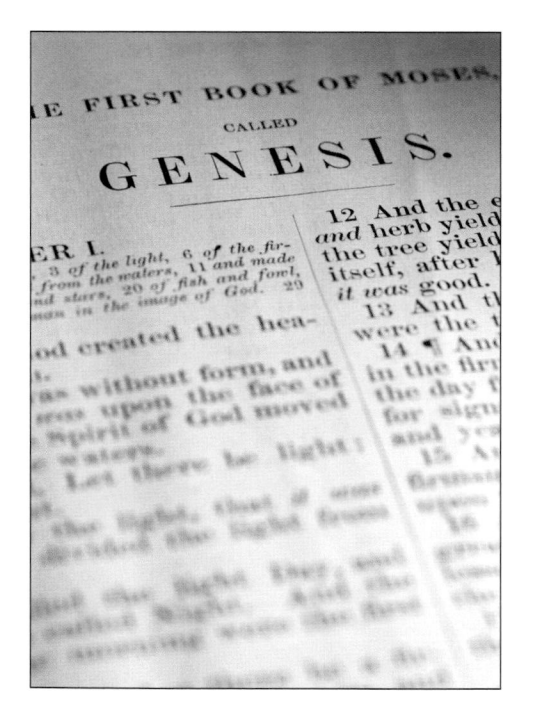

Some versions of the King James translation of the Bible have contained a marginal note referring to Bishop James Ussher's calculation that the creation took place in 4004 B.C.

The seamless blending of all knowledge

Charles Darwin, the man behind the **theory of evolution**, was born in 1809. If in that year a family in England had opened their King James Bible to the account of Genesis, they likely would have learned from a note printed in the margins that God had created the world in 4004 B.C. For those who took the Bible as authority, this meant the Earth was less than 6,000 years old. Printed as it was alongside the text of the Old Testament in the most common Bible of the time, this first date in a chronology of creation soon acquired the authority of scripture. But in fact, it had been calculated just 150 years earlier by an Irishman.

James Ussher (1581–1656), Archbishop of Armagh, was a keen scholar who traveled widely in his quest to collect information about ancient times. Before his death, he had acquired a library of more than 10,000 volumes. His *Annals of the World,* published in 1650, is a classic telling of the adventures of Abraham, Julius Caesar, Alexander the Great, and other characters of early history. His timeline of world events first appeared in this book.

Ussher used many different documents, including the Bible, to put together his list of dates. He also used careful reasoning. He calculated the year of creation by starting with the known dates of the reign of Nebuchadnezzar II and subtracting the life spans of the patriarchs as stated in the Bible. He inferred the month and day from the assumption that God's cre-

ation would harmonize with an astronomical beginning, such as an equinox or solstice. Given the biblical fact that the fruit was ripe in the Garden of Eden, Ussher deduced that creation must have occurred in autumn. He assumed that the first day of creation would have to have been a Sunday, because God rested on the seventh day and Saturday is the Hebrew day of rest. Using astronomical tables, Ussher was able to pinpoint the closest Sunday near the equinox of 4004, which led him to a specific date of October 23, beginning at sundown of the previous day.

Ussher's Annals of the World (1650) is where he first published his timeline of world events, including 4004 B.C. as the year of creation.

Ussher was a cleric who valued scholarship. He believed that the Bible contained no errors and therefore was at least as reliable as any other historical source. In typical fashion for scholars of his time, he seamlessly blended evidence from the Bible, history, and nature to understand his world.

The world as inferred from the Bible

Like Archbishop Ussher from a century and a half before, the average citizen at the opening of the 19th century understood the Bible as inspired by God and infallibly true. At that time, the dominant religious tradition across northwestern Europe was Protestantism, and a very influential brand of Protestantism was Calvinist. (Spain, France, and portions of Germany were largely Roman Catholic.) An important aspect of Calvinist Protestantism was the conviction that God was actively involved in all aspects of existence, everywhere, at every moment — that God suffused all activities and was ever-present. According to Calvinists, God worked from a plan, and the entire course of earthly events was preordained, including who would receive eternal life. An understanding of this plan could be obtained from the Bible and was especially explicit in the stories found in Genesis, the first book of the Old Testament.

In Genesis, God creates living kinds in a specific sequence. God started with grass, herbs, and plants; he then created fish and fowl; God then made creatures that walk and creep on the Earth; and finally, God made humankind. This was generally understood, in the early 1800s, to mean that God created each living kind in a unique act of **special creation**. God's command for the Earth to bring forth each creature "after his kind," sup-

In Genesis, God creates living things in a sequence beginning with plants and ending with humankind.

ported the sense of a fixed, unchangeable status for each species.[2]

According to Genesis, at the end of six days of creative activity, "God saw every thing that he had made, and behold, it was very good." For most Christians of this era, God worked alone to direct the creation, was actively involved in that creation, had created living things in their ideal forms, and was benevolent.

Genesis also was read to imply that human beings held a special place in creation because they were made last, were given dominion over the Earth and its creatures, and were created in God's image. The Old Testament, together with the New Testament descriptions of the life, works, death, and resurrection of Jesus, conveyed the idea that humans were essential to the creation, having been formed at the beginning and continuing until the end of time and beyond.

The order of the world described in Genesis dovetailed with a worldview from ancient Greece that was revived and adopted by Christians in the Middle Ages. This was the concept, dating back to ancient Greece, of a **great chain of being**. In this conception, all living things fall into a single, linear order that ascends from worms to human beings. Each link in this chain represents a species, and each has its own ideal structure and function.

Christian scholars elaborated on the original metaphor. They extended the chain up to God, with angels and archangels between humankind and the Creator. Some even proposed that evil spirits were links on the chain, slightly above humans and thus having the power to torment them. In any event, the many links to the chain, each slightly different from the next in a gradually ascending hierarchy, constituted evidence of God's perfect design, wisdom, and power. The image of a chain also inferred God's method of creation: that God had started with simpler organisms and link by individual link had worked up to the creation of humanity.

Natural philosophy and natural theology

In the centuries leading up to the 1800s, people who sought to make sense of the world around them — to uncover the underlying truth of nature — were known as **natural philosophers**. This tradition of thought dated back to the early Greeks and the Ionians before them. Natural philosophers sought information about the world so that they could better understand the nature of existence. They used logical reasoning and observation and (increasingly in the 1600s) experimentation as ways to learn about the workings of the world, the structure of the universe, and the origins of living things. By the 19th century, experimentation also had become an important source for information about the natural world.

For those natural philosophers within the Christian tradition, the pursuit of knowledge was a means of offering reverence to God and attaining greater understanding of God through God's works. This approach was captured in the metaphor of the two books: the Book of Scripture and the Book of Nature. Many intellectuals thought of God as the author of both books, and they considered the two as distinct but equivalent sources of the truth; the knowledge each contained was consistent with that of the other and did not conflict.

This point of view had been promoted by Augustine of Hippo (354–430), the fifth century bishop living in Roman North Africa and an influential writer on Christian doctrine. According to Augustine, any alleged points of difference could only be caused by human ignorance and misinterpretation. He rejected the idea that the biblical account of the world was truer than any account based on careful observation of nature. He cautioned Christians not to make such claims or they would bring ridicule on the Church. Augustine wrote:

> Even a non-Christian knows something about the Earth, the heavens, and the other elements of this world, about the motion and orbit of the stars and even their size and relative positions, about the predictable eclipses of the sun and moon, the cycles of the years and the seasons, about the kinds of animals, shrubs, stones, and so forth, and this knowledge he holds with certainty from reason and experience. It is thus offensive and disgraceful for an unbeliever to hear a Christian talk nonsense about such things, claiming that what he is saying is based on Scripture. We should do all that we can to avoid such an embarrassing situation, which people see as ignorance in the Christian and laugh to scorn.[3]

Augustine's argument for equivalency between the "two books" resonated down through the centuries. It was echoed by Francis Bacon (1561–1626), the English philosopher who is considered one of the founders of modern science for his ardent promotion of **inductive reasoning** — the building of scientific theories from facts and observations rather than through pure deductive reasoning built upon self-evident truth or "first principles." In his 1605 work *The Advancement of Learning,* Bacon wrote that a human being cannot "search too far or be too well-studied in the book of God's word, or in the book of God's works, divinity or philosophy; but rather let men endeavor an endless progress or proficiency in both."[4]

The astronomer Galileo Galilei (1564–1642) also advocated the idea that truth is found in the Bible *and* in nature. Galileo endorsed the Copernican hypothesis of a sun-centered universe, and by so doing, he brought upon himself the wrath of church authorities who believed it contradicted the biblical representation of the Earth as the center of God's universe. Galileo argued that the Bible's references to complex physical phenomena are incidental to its main purpose and are conveyed in simple, nonliteral ways so that all may understand. By contrast, he argued, the divine laws of nature operate without exception whether or not any human understands them. "For the Bible is not chained in every expression to conditions as strict as those which govern all physical effects," Galileo wrote in 1615, "nor is God any less excellently revealed in Nature's actions than in the sacred statements of the Bible." According to Galileo, the Bible is "the dictate of the Holy Ghost" and nature is "the observant executrix of God's commands."[5]

Galileo argued that knowledge of nature could influence how the Bible should be interpreted.

The "two books" were sometimes twined together into a position that came to be called the **argument from design** or **natural theology**. This is the position that evidence of order in the universe (such as the discovery of natural laws) is evidence for the existence of God. The English archdeacon William Paley (1743–1805) authored one of the most influential works in this vein. His book, *Natural Theology: Or, Evidences for the Existence and Attributes of the Deity, Collected from the Appearances of Nature,* was published just as the 19th century opened.

In this two-volume work, which became a standard textbook of the era, Paley employed the classic analogy of a watch and a watchmaker. If a person discovered a watch lying upon the ground, he would not assume that it had lain there forever. Rather, he would know, based on its complex workings, that it had been designed by someone for some purpose. Paley wrote that "there must have existed, at some time and at some place or other, an artificer or artificers who formed it for the purpose which we find it actually to answer, who comprehended its construction and designed its use." The same must be assumed for the even more complex objects that can be found in nature, Paley argued. He maintained that the "artificer" of such objects was God.

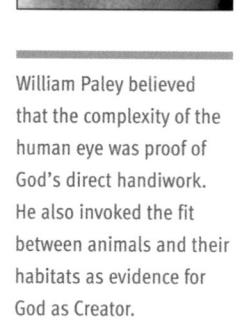

William Paley believed that the complexity of the human eye was proof of God's direct handiwork. He also invoked the fit between animals and their habitats as evidence for God as Creator.

For Paley, an obvious example of God's handiwork was the human eye, with its complex arrangement of lens, retina, and other interdependent parts. The theologian also pointed to the perfect fit between animals and their environments, such as the suitability of bird wings for flying and of fish fins for swimming. He perceived a perfect unity between the organic and the inorganic worlds. In this perfection, Paley saw a benevolent and compassionate God.

An alternative to Paley's interpretation was proposed by Richard Owen (1804–1892), a contemporary of Charles Darwin (1809–1882). Rather than focusing on the seemingly divine fit between species and their environments, Owen drew attention to what he saw as an overarching plan operating in nature. From his expertise as an anatomist, Owen documented the uncanny structural similarities that could be found across a variety of animal species. For example, the arm of a human, the limb of a dog, and the clawed foot of a bird all share similar arrangements of bone. To Owen, these **homologies** were evidence that God worked from templates, using ideal types to create the diversity of life on Earth.

Natural theology had its critics. Some theologians argued that it did not contribute to the understanding of God's *ultimate* purposes. They also asserted that while evidence of God found in nature might buttress the faith of believers, it would not convince nonbelievers. Some wondered how disease, natural disaster, and the like reflected God's good intentions. Despite such concerns, natural theology had an overwhelming influence on scientific scholarship well into the 19th century. It motivated investigators in many fields to look for God's design as evidence of God's benevolence. British geologist William Buckland (1784–1856) spoke for many when he said that in the various sciences "when fully understood ... will be found a potent and consistent auxiliary" to revealed religion, "exalting our conviction of the Power, and Wisdom, and Goodness of the Creator."[6]

An evolving sense of history

For centuries, it had been assumed that the first five books of the Old Testament of the Bible, known as the Pentateuch, had been dictated to Moses by God. But beginning in the middle of the 18th century, Biblical scholars belonging to the school of learning that has been called **higher criticism** began to suggest that these books had more than one author. As historical and literary analysis of the Bible continued to develop, scholars proposed that the Pentateuch had been pieced together from several distinct oral traditions and manuscripts. They noted that many biblical stories, including the creation story in Genesis, were repetitive and contained contradictions, style shifts, the use of different referents for "God," and other clues suggesting authors from different time periods and cultural contexts. They noted also that the New Testament Gospels gave four significantly different accounts of the life of Jesus.

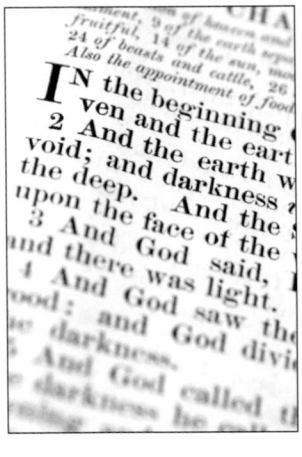

In the 18th and 19th centuries, historians began to apply the same forms of analysis of historical documents to the text of the Bible, with particular attention to understanding who the authors were, who their audiences were, and the particular forms of literary expression that were used by the authors.

Among scholarly theologians in the 1800s, therefore, there was a growing sense that the biblical narrative was told from not one but a variety of perspectives. In other words, the Bible's truth could not be a literal truth. Rather, the Bible conveyed a truth that was textured, complex, subject to interpretation, and having to do with salvation, rather than truth about nature. Another idea that emerged through this scholarship was that God revealed the truth gradually to people as they are able to comprehend it; as they obtained a greater understanding of the natural world, their sense of the meaning of the Bible would become subtle and richer. This was called the **principle of accommodation**.

©Haines Photo Co, Library of Congress

Such new views concerning the formation of the Bible, while emanating from Christian scholars, were not easily accepted by ordinary clergy and the general public. Free-thinkers, rationalists, and atheists who already doubted the authority of the Bible used this scholarship to advance their points of view, adding to the religious anxiety and cultural debate that continued throughout the 19th century.

Rapid social change and the spread of affluence resulting from the Industrial Revolution encouraged the idea of historical progress in contrast to a view of the world as static.

Meanwhile, the scholars examining the historical nature of the Bible also had begun to look at other classical texts in the same way. Through their work, they began to challenge the widely held belief that the Earth and its living forms had remained unchanged since the original creation and that if any change had occurred, it was degeneration from perfection. With the advance in historical scholarship, the traditional belief in a static, unchanging world was slowly replaced by the idea that the world in all its parts had come into being gradually, that life on Earth had gone through changes, and the changes constituted progress. The emergence of the Industrial Age in the 18th and 19th centuries, which brought new comfort and affluence to a much larger share of the population than ever before (though by no means to everyone), reinforced this sense of historical progress for those who benefited from it.

At about the same time, geologists — and the theologians who kept up with scientific learning — were moving away from the idea that the Earth was a mere 6,000 years old and had been initially formed in its present form in a single week of creation. They began to adopt a more dynamic perspective that allowed for ongoing changes over a much longer span of time. This allowed them to explain the geological formations that had been discovered. It also raised new questions for religious thinkers of the 19th century. How should they interpret the days of the first chapter of Genesis? Perhaps each day symbolized an entire epoch; this suggestion came to be termed the **day-age theory**. Or perhaps there was an immense gap of time between

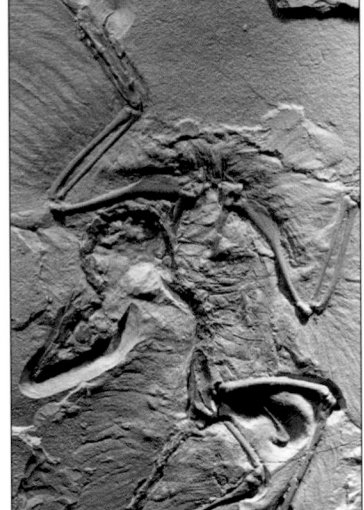

(Top) The first intact *Archaeopteryx lithographica* fossil was discovered in 1861.

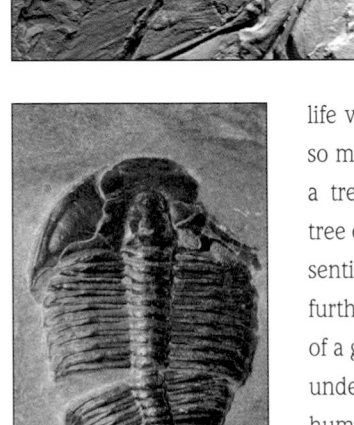

(Bottom) Although the first trilobite fossil was discovered in 1648, large numbers were uncovered during the mining of limestone for use in production of steel.

an initial creation referred to in Genesis 1:1 and the six-day creation described in the rest of the chapter; this in turn was called the **gap theory**.

The new questions about the Earth's age had been triggered by advances in the geological sciences that themselves had been spurred by excavations of industry. All that digging into the Earth had brought forth an unprecedented number of fossils. Analysis of these fossils along with analysis of specimens of living species led to the idea that life was not organized in a ladder formation so much as in a branching arrangement, like a tree. Furthermore, this newly conceived tree of life had many clipped branches, representing extinct species. This new evidence further discredited the old and fading notion of a great chain of being. At the same time, it undermined the corollary assumption that humanity was God's ultimate creation.

Another question generated by the fossils was the mystery about the fate of species that were preserved in rock but not found in living form on Earth. Geologists were divided between two schools of thought. According to one school, major events and in particular Noah's flood as described in Genesis had formed the Earth's present-day geology and wiped out earlier species (now fossils). According to the other school, common natural processes in operation over great spans of time created small, steady, and gradual change in the geology of the Earth. Under such a view, some sort of **organic succession** (changes in species over time) must have occurred. Both geological scenarios required Christians to revisit Genesis and consider what, exactly, the text meant when it described the creation of the world.

Of all the changing sensibilities that marked the 19th century, one of the most important was that concerning the pursuit of knowledge. There was an emerging conviction that scientific explanations should rely only on **empirical evidence** — on what can be learned through observation of the natural world. The practitioners of science increasingly sought to insulate their pursuit of knowledge about nature from the influence of their own religious, social, or cultural beliefs. Evidence from observation or experimentation would guide their conclusions. Toward the end of the 1800s, they began to call themselves scientists to distinguish themselves from philosophers or theologians who speculated about metaphysical matters or supernatural involvement in the natural world. By the end of that century, the general consensus among western scientists, most of whom were Christians, was to keep religious speculation and faith statements outside of and separate from their empirical studies and scientific conclusions.

Darwin's religious views

In the continuum of belief extending from the orthodox Christianity of his time to atheism, Darwin hovered somewhere in between. His father, Robert Darwin (1766–1848), and especially his grandfather Erasmus Darwin (1731–1802), were freethinkers, believing in God but not in the authority of organized religion nor in a literal reading of the Bible. Charles married his cousin, Emma Wedgwood (1808–1896), who was religious but not in the Calvinist vein. Rather, she was Unitarian, a tradition characterized by tolerance, rationalism, and a focus on universal moral values.

Darwin's writings, and biographies about him, draw a portrait of an extremely sensitive, gentle man who throughout his entire life was enthralled with nature, both by its majestic sweep and in its minutest details. His awe could be termed religious, and yet he did not subscribe to the Christian doctrines of revelation, redemption, and salvation. Darwin reportedly had trouble accepting a belief system according to which people he so admired, such as his own father and grandfather, were destined for Hell because of their lack of orthodoxy. Some historians have shown that a primary obstacle to his acceptance of a personally involved and benevolent God was the illness and death of his beloved 10-year-old daughter Annie.

Darwin was affected not only by the very personal tragedy with Annie, but also by the infinite amount of waste and death that he realized must occur through **natural selection**, the mechanism he considered the primary driver of evolution. Natural selection is a term that describes how individuals in a species most adapted to their environment are more likely to survive, reproduce, and pass on their adaptive characteristics to the next generation. In correspondence with others, Darwin admitted that the religious implications of natural selection "staggered" him and that the theological problems it raised were "painful" to him.[7]

Part of Darwin's ambivalence about the concept of a God who created the world and was at work in it stemmed from his distrust in the human ability to comprehend the true nature of existence. He spoke to others of being drawn, almost instinctively, toward the belief in a God who originated the world — to a **First Cause**. More than once he said or wrote to others that he could not believe that the world as it existed was the result of evolutionary processes alone. "But then with me the horrid doubt always arises," he once stated, "whether the convictions of man's mind, which has been developed from the mind of the lower animals, are of any value or at all trustworthy. Would anyone trust in the convictions of a monkey's mind, if there are any convictions in such a mind?"[8] As he put it in another correspondence, "I feel most deeply that the whole subject is too profound for the human intellect. A dog might as well speculate on the mind of Newton. Let each man hope and believe what he can."[9]

Late in Darwin's life, a schoolteacher wrote to ask his opinion on the origin of life and God's role in it. Darwin wrote her back: "I hardly know what to say. Though no evidence worth anything has, as yet, in my opinion, been advanced in favor of a living being being developed from inorganic matter, yet I cannot avoid believing the possibility of this will be proved some day in accordance with the law of continuity. If it is ever found that life can originate on this world, the vital phenomena will come under some general law of nature. Whether the existence of a conscious God can be proved from the existence of the so-called laws of nature ... is a perplexing subject, one which I have often thought, but cannot see my way clearly."[10]

And so, while Darwin never denied the existence of God, he could never fully embrace God, either. "I think that generally, and more and more as I grow older, but not always," he wrote, "that an agnostic would be the most correct description of my state of mind."[11]

FURTHER READING

God and Nature: Historical essays on the encounter between Christianity and science, David C. Lindberg and Ronald L. Numbers, eds. (University of California Press, 1986)

When Science and Christianity Meet, David C. Lindberg and Ronald L. Numbers, eds. (University of California Press, 2003)

The theory of evolution

"You're just in time!" exclaimed Dr. Laurel Dunbar as Angela Rawlett entered her advisor's cramped office. The biology professor was holding the bracket for a bookshelf in her right hand and a screw gun in her left. "I just can't reach above my desk to put this up. I've got to get these plants off my desk! They're ruining my papers."

The younger but taller woman took over with the screw gun. Dr. Dunbar picked a plant off her desk and settled back into a chair. "So," she said to Angela's back, "How is Bio 122 going?"

"The evolution class? I like it. Dr. Brown is a good lecturer. But I was right, too. I do have a problem with evolution. It's too gruesome."

"Red in tooth and claw, hmm?" the professor murmured.

Angela turned around with a puzzled look. "I'm talking about the competition for survival. According to your theory of evolution, more organisms are born than can live. Not to mention wholesale extinction of species. Isn't it all so heartless?" She turned back to the wall, jammed the screw gun against a pencil mark and drilled. She did not see Dr. Dunbar nod her head.

"There's a family of geese living in the lake across from the campus center," Dr. Dunbar said as she caressed the leaves of the plant in her lap. "Five goslings hatched about a month ago. Last week there were only four. Today … two."

"That proves my point!" Angela exclaimed as she aimed the screw gun at a second mark. "If God wanted that pair of geese to have only two goslings, why not give them two to start? Why would he set up nature to be so cruel?"

The larvae of the Ichneumon wasp, hatched within the stomach of a caterpillar, feed off their paralyzed living host as they develop.

The professor nodded again. "Cruel. Heartless. We could use those words to describe the process. But we must also remember that's what bad for the goose is good for the fox."

Angela turned around. "What fox?"

"I'm assuming that the goslings didn't drown," the professor answered as she handed Angela anchors to place in the screw holes. "Possibly they died of disease, but just as likely, some predator got them. So from the fox's point of view, nature is bountiful."

Angela frowned, but the professor gave a reassuring smile. "I don't mean to belittle your concerns," she said. "Charles Darwin was just as sensitive. Have you ever heard of the Ichneumon wasp?" The student shook her head.

"It lays its eggs in the stomach of a caterpillar that it has paralyzed with its stings. The larvae feed off the insides of their still-living host. That's a lot worse than the case of our disappearing goslings. That wasp made Darwin wonder what kind of God could have created such a world."

"Well, I wonder, too," Angela said emphatically.

"Don't let that keep you from finishing this job," responded Dr. Dunbar. The student drilled two holes for the other bracket, inserted the anchors, screwed the brackets into place, and set the shelf on top of them. "Why, though?" Angela asked. "Why do we have to have this survival-of-the-fittest kind of world?"

"Speaking as a scientist, I cannot answer the question of why we live in an imperfect world where death and destruction coexist with life and beauty," her advisor responded. "I can only attempt to figure out what happens in this world and how nature produces the results it does."

The professor paused, then added, "You know, Darwin once stepped outside his scientific self to offer a justification. That might be of interest to you." She reached to a bookcase next to her and handed her student a worn paperback copy of *The Origin of Species*. "Turn to the last sentence and read it to me," she said.

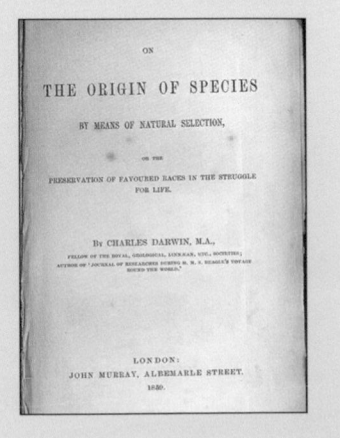

ON

THE ORIGIN OF SPECIES

BY MEANS OF NATURAL SELECTION,

OR THE
PRESERVATION OF FAVOURED RACES IN THE STRUGGLE
FOR LIFE.

By CHARLES DARWIN, M.A.,

LONDON:
JOHN MURRAY, ALBEMARLE STREET.

"'There is a grandeur in this view of life,'" Angela read, "'with its several powers, having been originally breathed by the Creator into a few forms or into one; and that, whilst this planet has gone cycling on according to the fixed laws of gravity, from so simple a beginning endless forms most beautiful and most wonderful have been and are being evolved.'"

The professor took the plant from her lap and handed it to Angela to place on the newly hung shelf. "Lamb's ear. Very soft to touch. This one," she said, picking another small pot off her desk, "is aloe vera. Prickly, but with a soothing gel inside. And here," she said, picking up a third pot, "is lavender. Used to ward off the plague in medieval times. So very fragrant." She handed the lavender to Angela. "Three of the hundreds of thousands of plant species in this world. What do you think?"

"Endless forms most beautiful," the student quoted as she sniffed the lavender. "There is grandeur with the gruesome. I'll admit that much."

"Endless forms most beautiful."

CHAPTER 3

The theory of evolution

New fossil finds are providing insight into the relationships between extinct species like the dinosaurs and their modern biological heirs, the birds.

Evolution in action

Sometimes it helps to understand an idea by starting with examples. Here are three stories that demonstrate the theory of evolution:

Story 1. The fossil of a small, duck-sized dinosaur is curled up in a position eerily similar to that taken by birds when they are sleeping or resting. Named *Mei long* for "soundly sleeping dragon," this fossil was discovered in Northeastern China in 2004. *Mei long* lies on folded hind limbs, encircled by its long tail, with its head turned backward and tucked between its forearm and trunk. It was unearthed from a region that in the same year produced another extraordinary fossil: *Dilong paradoxus*, ancestor of the notoriously fearsome *Tyrannosaurus rex*. In contrast to the oversize *T. Rex*, the fossil of *Dilong paradoxus* is as small as a wolf, with fine, hair-like feathers detailed on its limbs. Fossils like these, sharing characteristics of both dinosaurs and birds, have been discovered at locations around the world and are helping to clarify the evolutionary relationship between extinct and living animals.

Story 2. Before "Johnny Appleseed" (John Chapman, 1774–1845) and others like him introduced apple trees across America, there was a maggot fly that laid its eggs on hawthorn berries. At some point, a maggot fly must have tested out an apple as a maternity ward and found that it worked, because today the maggot fly lays its eggs on both apple and hawthorn. Individual flies have their preferences. Females typically return to lay their eggs,

Evolution Dialogues

and males tend to look for mates, on the fruit that birthed them. Though such flies could mate with each other — an apple-born fly with a hawthorn berry-born fly, for example — they tend not to because they don't cross paths as much. In a span of less than 200 years, these two populations of maggot fly have begun to diverge. Scientists believe that as these two populations continue to follow separate paths, differences will evolve that prevent the two groups from successfully mating even when brought together. When that occurs, scientists will know that speciation has taken place; in other words, that a new species has branched off from an existing species. Researchers are documenting many instances of such speciation underway in both plants and animals.

Story 3. In a recent experiment, researchers placed a dozen populations of the same strain of bacterium, *P. fluorescens*, in a laboratory vessel along with a parasite virus. After just 50 generations, genetic variation between the bacteria populations increased significantly. Each had evolved in a unique manner to resist the parasite. In another experiment, researchers abundantly supplied glucose to a flask containing *E. coli* bacteria. The bacteria grew well but with the population increase, competition developed for the food source. Some of the bacteria won the

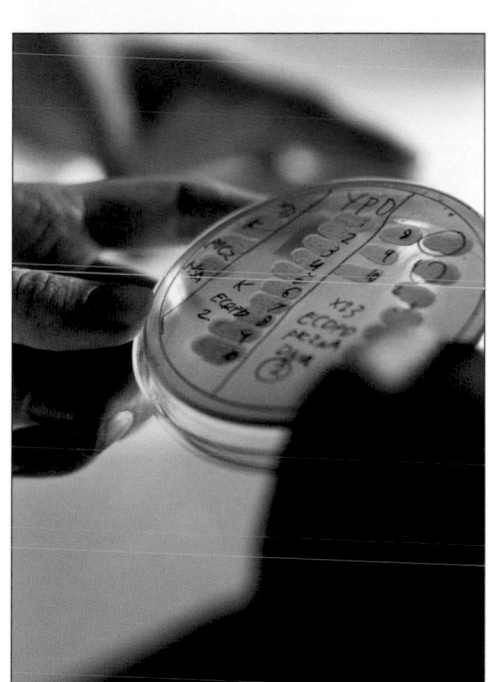

competition for the glucose, while the rest evolved in such a way that they could feed off the by-products from the initial glucose consumption. These experiments are among the growing number of lab-based projects that enable scientists to observe evolution in real time. Bacteria can replicate in days or even hours, and the environment inside a Petri dish or flask can be restricted to a few variables. The lab experiments are a means of testing the theory of evolution, something that is more difficult to do in the natural world, where ecosystems such as a jungle or lake bottom are immensely complex and the process of speciation takes many thousands of years.

Studies of organisms as diverse as fruit trees, flies, and bacteria are demonstrating evolution in action today.

These three examples illustrate the variety of ways that scientists today are accumulating evidence to test the theory of evolution. They are analyzing artifacts from the past, observing species in nature, and conducting experiments in the laboratory. The theory of evolution is not merely an abstract, hypothetical idea, but an essential framework guiding research today. But what is it, exactly? What is "evolution"?

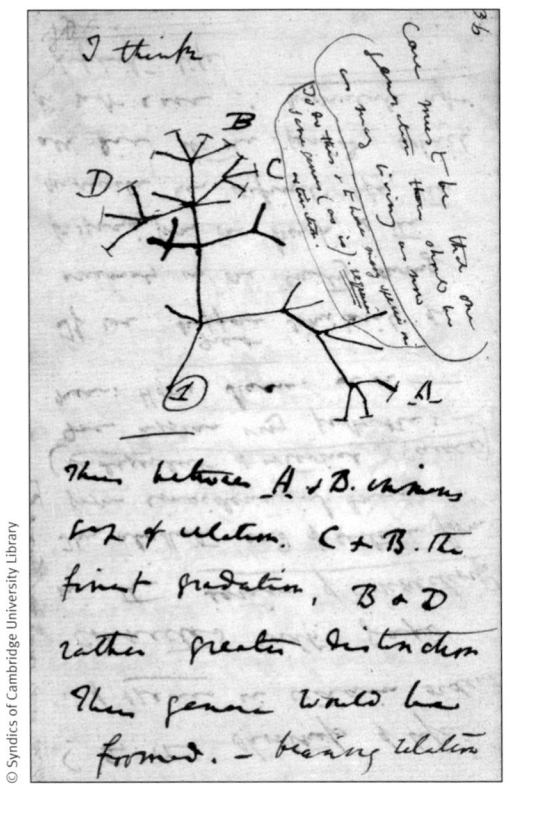

Darwin's notes include this sketch of an evolutionary "tree."

Unlike string theory or quantum theory, it is easy to quickly grasp the essentials of evolutionary theory. The 19th century scientist Charles Darwin (1809–1882) summed it up in just three words: *descent with modification.* The forms of life that populate the Earth have changed over time and continue to change. Furthermore, all species living and extinct are related to each other. From one or a very few common ancestors way back in time, the great diversity of life has emerged.

Through the process of evolution, each species becomes distinct from the rest through the accumulation of many small, incremental changes to traits, handed down through different lines of descendants over millions of years. A species can change so much over the generations that it becomes a new species. Much more commonly, one or more new species branch off from an existing species that itself continues to evolve. Species go into decline and extinction even as others emerge or thrive. Evolution is a living process, often depicted as the "tree of life," though the branching growth of new species from and alongside older species is denser and more tangled than any real tree or bush.

Natural selection

There are several engines that drive evolution, but the most important one (and the one emphasized by Charles Darwin) is **natural selection**. For any given trait, whether it be wing color or leg strength or brain power, there are variants that are more advantageous compared to others in a particular environment. Those who bear the more adaptive trait or combinations of traits are more likely to survive and reproduce than those who don't. Over many generations, the adaptive variants flourish within a species.

Natural selection is not random. What is random is the introduction of minute changes into the **DNA**, the molecular code that is inherited and passed on from one generation to the next. Certain of these chance variations, called **mutations**, produce changes

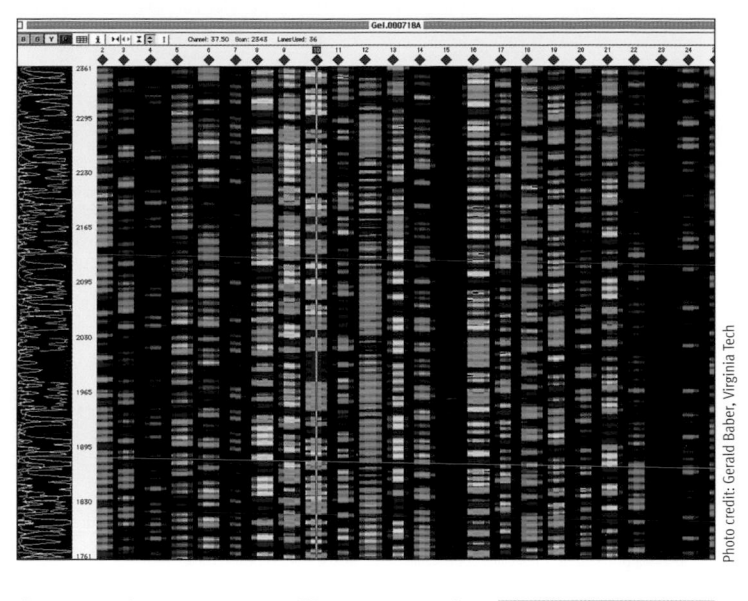

Photo credit: Gerald Baber, Virginia Tech

Color displays, like that above, produced by contemporary DNA sequencing technology, allow researchers to identify the genetic structure of an organism.

to traits that result in better fitness to the environment. These traits and their underlying mutations are the ones that tend to endure through the generations.

Mutations may be introduced into an organism at any point along its DNA inside any cell at any time in life. Mutations can be triggered by radiation, malnutrition, aging, and physical trauma to the cell. However, most mutations do not result from any external triggers. Instead, they occur naturally when cells replicate themselves. At statistically consistent intervals of about once every million replications, errors are introduced. If a mutation occurs in a sperm or egg cell involved in reproduction, then the altered DNA sequence and whatever effects it may have passes on to the next generation.

Variation is also introduced into a species through **recombination**. This is the complex process by which the sperm and egg cells are created with a different genetic makeup than the originating parental cells. In other words, the DNA is reshuffled each generation so that a different hand of genetic cards are dealt to each offspring.

Most changes to the DNA have no effect or only subtle, minor effects. A rare few result in a dramatic change to function, appearance, or behavior. Some of these rare mutations are harmful and reduce the likelihood that an organism will survive. A very few are **adaptive**; they cause a change in the organism that improves its ability to survive or reproduce compared to organisms without this mutation.

DNA changes, therefore, are the means by which new traits are introduced into a population. For example, an eagle with slightly better distance

vision compared to other eagles has a greater likelihood of surviving and passing on its genetic inheritance. The chances of the eagle with superior and inferior distance vision are not even — they are not random. The changes preserved through natural selection are the ones that provide advantage.

Though an individual has at most two versions of any gene, a population can possess many more. This collective assortment of all versions for all genes is the **gene pool** of the population. A population evolves when its gene pool changes. This change is measured in the frequency of particular versions of genes in the whole population over time, with some alleles more or less frequent than before, others disappearing entirely, or new ones emerging.

In a stable environment, a species may evolve so many adaptive traits that it seems to fit perfectly. Such a well-adapted species might change very little over millennia so long as the environment stays the same. Its gene pool will stay relatively static; traits that have proven successful continue to trump the new mutations that are constantly being introduced. This explains why the basic body shape of sharks have endured for some 425 million years. They are supremely fit to the ocean environment that has remained relatively constant over millennia.

In a changing environment, a species may evolve relatively quickly and dramatically. Adaptations that worked before may no longer aid survival. New mutations and the traits they effect may come into dominance. This explains why strains of HIV virus are evolving so rapidly in response to anti-AIDS medicines. Mutations that enhance resistance to the drugs become concentrated in surviving generations.

If a species does not generate and preserve adaptive mutations in response to a changing environment, it may go extinct. This helps explain why smallpox has been eliminated from the natural world. Vaccines made the human body an inhospitable environment more quickly than the virus could generate adaptive mutations. The virus is not extinct, however; inside research labs, small populations are kept in artificial environments to which it is still adapted.

Other evolutionary mechanisms

Scientists have demonstrated that there are other mechanisms besides natural selection that drive evolution. One of them is **sexual selection**. This is a process by which traits may increase reproductive success even at the expense of long-term survival. When male elk emit their bugle calls and clash antlers in a contest to see who will mate, they risk injury and death, but the dominant bulls from these contests mate with the most females. Elk females pay close attention to the rutting contests of the males, and they vie for the opportunity to mate with the winners. Through these behaviors, the dominant animals of both genders transfer more of their DNA to the next generation.

Some species have characteristics that seem to be disadvantageous for survival (e.g., the male peacock's plumage or the male elk rutting combat) but that play an important role in enhancing the possibility of reproduction.

In many species, the males (and in a few species, the females) compete for the attention of prospective mates with dominance displays, brilliant colors, complex calls and warbles, displays of plumage, or other physical shows. A peacock's tail may seem a superficial reason for choosing a mate, but it's actually rational according to research, because males with the biggest, flashiest, and most symmetric displays of feathers tend to be the healthiest. Members of the population that are less impressive may survive to reproductive maturity, but they are selected as mates less often, and so

Genetic drift is caused by random events that alter the environmental context and isolate a portion of a genetic population.

they contribute less to the gene pool of future generations.

Another important evolutionary mechanism is **genetic drift**, or random changes in the frequency of alleles from generation to generation. This agent of evolution did not occur to Charles Darwin when he was developing his theory, but scientists today understand it is a significant contributor to species change.

Genetic drift is sometimes caused by significant changes to the environment. A landslide that creates a rift down a mountainside, cleaving a population of mammals in two; a sudden strong shift in wind current that divides a flock of birds: these kinds of natural events can cause a change in the genetic makeup of a population.

A different form of genetic drift is caused by migration. When rats boarded ships in the Old World and then disembarked in the New World, genetic drift occurred. The new colonies of rats started up by the handful of rats that went ashore at various ports each started with a much smaller gene pool compared to that back in their home country.

The key element of genetic drift is chance, not fitness. Yet genetic drift is not rare, particularly in small populations. It happens all the time. Each autumn when an oak tree sheds its acorns, only a few (and not necessarily the "best") actually fall on fertile soil and are not eaten by squirrels, mowed over, or squashed by a car tire. Only a very few (again, not necessarily the "most fit") survive all the vicissitudes of life to someday produce their own acorns. The same play of chance affects everything and everyone that is born, from the thousands of eggs that a frog lays each season to the millions of humans born on any day across the Earth. The genes of those who by chance survive random events that killed off others move forward to the next generation.

Genetic drift also occurs when circumstantial events cause the relatively sudden influx of genes from one population into another. If some of the rats from Europe, mentioned above, disembarked at one wharf on the American coastline and others got off at a wharf a few miles upriver, two new communities of rats would each grow from very small gene pools. But if these populations of rats became so large that they spread across each other's territories and interbred, their joint gene pool would become larger.

Not just animals but plants, too, can be affected by sudden changes to the gene pool. This occurs when, for example, wind or insects carry pollen from one field to another far away. Humans also facilitate the exchange of genes between populations of plants when they store harvests from different fields at the same granary. Another contemporary is the contamination of organic crops by genetically modified varieties. These accidental crosses are evidence for the ease with which genes can flow from one population into another.

Microevolution and macroevolution

Small-scale evolutionary changes are referred to as **microevolution**. This is the easily observable process by which organisms change within a species. We see evidence for microevolution in the immense variety of dog breeds. From a common canine ancestor — gray wolves that roamed the northern continents — the vast range of dog from Chihuahua to Great Dane has emerged. Yet all domestic dogs still belong to one species, *Canis lupus familiaris*, and are capable of interbreeding. Dog diversity has occurred through natural evolutionary processes but to an even greater degree through human intervention. People have been selectively breeding canines over thousands of years to create dogs of various size, color, appearance, hunting and scent-following abilities, and companionship quality. Breeders knew their techniques worked long before evolutionary theory was able to explain how they worked.

Microevolution also refers to changes that take place within a relatively short timeframe. Darwin thought that natural evolutionary effects were too gradual to be observed scientifically. For many years, most other scientists thought so, too. But a groundbreaking study of the finches of the Galapagos Islands helped overturn this assumption. The Galapagos finches had

The varieties of Galapagos finches intrigued Darwin when he visited the islands in 1835.

intrigued Darwin when he visited the islands in 1835. After returning to England, Darwin studied specimens collected by the crew from the H.M.S. Beagle. He noted that each island's finches had differently shaped beaks. This observation led him to the startling hypothesis that all of the birds were related and were descended from a single species of bird that long ago had flown to the empty islands from the coast of South America. Darwin hypothesized that through natural selection, the beaks of each island's birds had become adapted to the particular seeds and insects found on their particular island. He did not have any data to support this idea, however.

A long-term study conducted since 1973 by Peter and Rosemary Grant of Princeton University has provided microevolutionary evidence in support of Darwin's hypothesis. Over the years, the Grants have collected information on the physical features of the common ground finches of Galapagos, their food supply, and island weather conditions. Their data show that during times of drought, the finch beaks become thicker. This change is measurable in the short span of a few generations. The Grants hypothesize that the finches with bigger beaks are able to feed off a larger size range of seeds and so have a survival advantage over those finches that can only crack the smaller seeds. According to the Grants, even a difference of a half a millimeter gives a survival advantage in times of drought. Many studies of similar design centered on other species, such as the guppies of Trinidad and the tiny cichlids of Lake Victoria, also have documented in real time the power of natural selection to modify species.

Scientists use the word **macroevolution** to refer to the overall movements of change in the history of life. The great explosion of new species in the Cambrian Period 500 million years ago is a macroevolutionary event, as are the mass extinctions that occurred during the Permian and Triassic periods. Macroevolution is the convergence of many microevolutionary events. The study of the Galapagos Island finches has documented not only microevolutionary trends in beak size but also a macroevolutionary trend: a range of new species emerging from a single common ancestor. There are six different species of ground finch on the islands. Each species of ground finch is distinct in terms of behavior, appearance, and genetics. Yet occasionally, interbreeding takes place. The boundaries between these finch species are present but still porous. The six species have emerged and continue to diverge, each shaped by the accumulation of small changes triggered by evolutionary mechanisms.

It needs to be said here that "boundary" and "species" are human constructs: they describe the circles that humans draw around populations of like organisms in order to compare them to less similar populations. Discrete species do not exist in a historic sense, because evolution is a continual process. Along each line of descent, there is a continuum of creatures, each slightly different in genetic makeup and external attributes from its immediate ancestors and descendants.

The simplest definition scientists use to define species is a group of organisms that can reproduce successfully and does so commonly in the wild. When horses and donkeys mate, they produce mules, which are sterile and cannot reproduce. Therefore, horses and donkeys are separate species, though the two share many similarities. There are hundreds of varieties of fruit fly that to the naked eye look alike. However, each variety has different courtship behaviors and mating cycles and in the wild do not mate. For this reason, they are typically categorized as different species.

An original species and a new one that branches out from it may be separated geographically and not affect each other's survival. If they share the same territory, they may coexist harmoniously with each carving out its own niche or they may compete for resources. In cases where they do compete, one species may have more success and force the other into extinction.

The number of species on the Earth today that have been discovered and formally described is just 1.8 million, and scientists estimate that there are at least 4 million and perhaps a great many millions more. All of them are descended from a single-celled organism or population of such organisms that appeared on Earth around 3.8 billion years ago. From those organisms and through the course of many generations, species of living creatures branched out. From those branches, other species emerged, creating a "tree of life" that is in fact much more like a bush. Many species that have evolved have also disappeared; their branches do not lead to any further branching.

It is estimated that more than 99 percent of all species that have ever lived on Earth are now extinct. As one scientific writer has put it, the tree of life contains many ancestors but few descendants. To give one example: some four million years ago, a variety of **hominoid** species, ape and human, roamed the planet. Now only a handful survive, many of which are endangered.

Evidence for evolution

When Darwin first proposed his theory of evolution, he lacked much of the scientific knowledge we have today. Any number of discoveries could have come along to undermine some or all of his theory. But the opposite has happened. From a variety of scientific avenues, supporting evidence has mounted.

Darwin's idea of descent with modification has a crucial implication: that all forms of life are related to one another. Discoveries in chemistry and molecular biology now show how on target he was. The physical bodies of all living things are constructed from the same basic structural units or **cells**, comprised of the same basic molecules of amino acids, nucleotides, and sugars. These cells are more similar across species than they are dif-

Evidence for the common descent of all life is found in the substantial structural similarities of animal and plant cells.

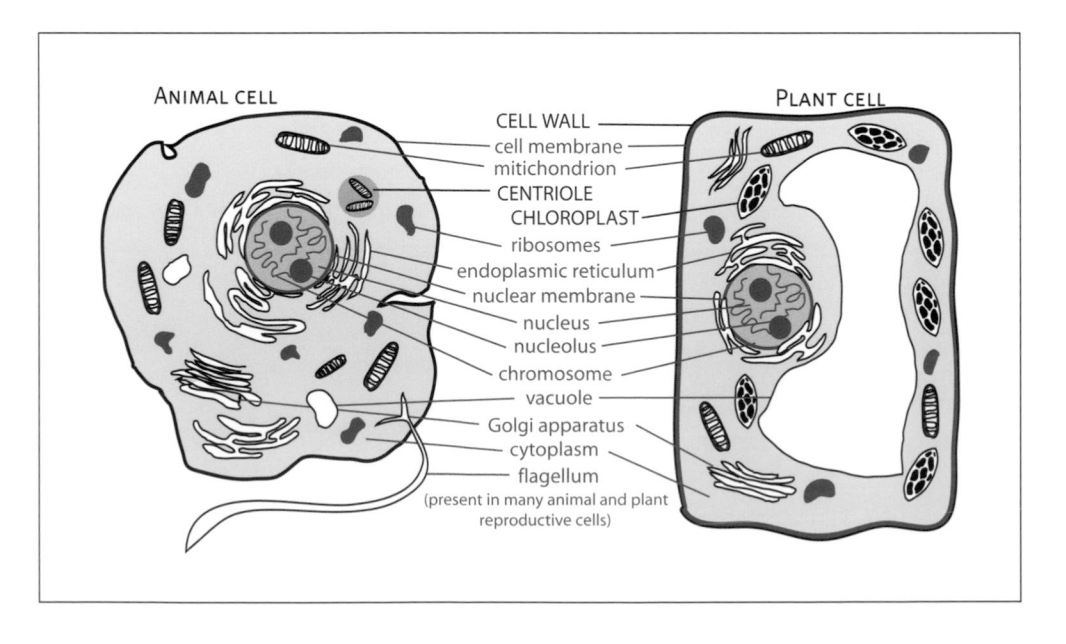

ANIMAL CELL
PLANT CELL

CELL WALL
cell membrane
mitichondrion
CENTRIOLE
CHLOROPLAST
ribosomes
endoplasmic reticulum
nuclear membrane
nucleus
nucleolus
chromosome
vacuole
Golgi apparatus
cytoplasm
flagellum
(present in many animal and plant reproductive cells)

Evolution Dialogues

ferent. All living things also rely on the same DNA and RNA, which carry and transfer the instructions for body construction and function. In fact, the immense variation required for natural selection to have its effects materializes in these strands of nucleic acids.

Homologies provide more evidence for relatedness. These are anatomical structures that bear resemblance across species. The forelimbs of the frog, the lizard, the rabbit, and the bird share the same humerus-radius-ulna arrangement of bones even though each kind uses its limbs quite differently. A prehistoric fish called *Eusthenopteron* also has this configuration in its forelimb. Many, many such homologies can be cited and hint at descent from a common ancestor.

Ostriches have wings like other birds but do not fly, while snakes and whales have pelvic bones they do not need, and certain species of cave fish have eyes but do not see. The presence of these vestigial parts is best explained by ancestry from an earlier species in which homologous parts had function.

Vestigal wings on ostriches and pelvic bones in snakes suggest that these creatures are descended from earlier species in which these features were functional.

Sometimes homologies are revealed in embryo. Baleen whales possess teeth in the early fetal stage but then lose them, unlike other whale species that retain their teeth throughout life. Humans and other land-based vertebrates have gill slits in embryo that do not develop. Many different kinds of organisms, from fruit flies to humans, have similar gene sequences active in early development and affecting body plan. The theory of evolution, with descent from a common ancestor, elegantly explains such mysteries.

Another aspect of evolutionary theory is that from a common ancestor way back in time, the diversity of life has emerged in a process of incremental change. The prediction that follows is that fossils should be found corresponding to the various stages of transformation. When Darwin first made his theory back in 1859, few so-called **transitional fossils** had been found. But today, thousands of such fossils have been recovered, from all across Earth and from points all across the billion years since life first emerged.

Transitional fossils collectively reflect three kinds of change. The first is the process of change within species. A great many such fossils have been

found. As but one example, the paleontologists Glenn A. Goodfriend (1951–2002) and Stephen Jay Gould (1941–2002) have tracked the transformations over 15,000–20,000 years in one particular species of land snail found in the Bahamas.

Transitional fossils also have been found that, when lined up, demonstrate broader cross-species change. Using transitional fossils, scientists have been able to reconstruct the evolution from early horse species characterized by four toes on each foot to later horse species with single-toed hooves. As another example of cross-species change, fossils have been found that illustrate the fine-grained changes to the ear and ribs of scallop shells across a time frame of more than 13 million years. These are just two of hundreds of other examples.

The third kind of change documented by transitional fossils is change across the lines that separate organisms of one type of body plan from another. A sufficient number of such fossils have been found to document the evolutionary line that descends from primitive jawless fish to

Many fossils demonstrate change from one body type to another; the example above is an intermediary from between dinosaurs and birds.

The fossils of certain plants and animals (e.g., like the moths shown at right) are rare because their habitats were not in or near bodies of water and they did not have hard body parts.

sharks, skates, and rays; from early land mammals to whales; from dinosaurs to birds; from early primates to modern *Homo sapiens*; and down through many other lines of macroevolutionary change.

Contemporary excavations are yielding many exciting and significant contributions to the fossil record. However, scientists do not ever expect to have enough fossils to draw a complete pictorial record of descent with modification. There are many reasons for this. One is that only organisms with hard body parts such as shell or bone are preserved through fossilization. Another reason is that fossils are only preserved where sediment builds up to cover dead bodies, such as on an ocean floor or lakebed. As a result, certain kinds of plants and animals, such as those of forests, are much more rare compared to those of organisms that dwelled in or near water. A third reason is that many fossils that were created millions of years ago have since been damaged or destroyed by geological events.

Taken as a whole, however, the fossil record justifies Darwin's theory in another way. Descent with modification suggests a timeline of change, and so it stands to reason that fossils of the earliest and most primitive organisms would be found at the deepest layers of the Earth, while the diversity that has sprung from them would be more abundant with each succeeding layer. And that is what has been found.

Where the rock layers have been undisrupted, fossils appear in a time progression and in a definite sequential order. **Trilobites** are found in vast quantities in rock that date back 250 million years or more, but not in more recent layers. Dinosaur fossils are found in rock between about 250 million and 65 million years old, but not in rock older or younger. Human fossils are found only in the top rock layers. The order of fossils is consistent from location to location, with particular combinations of fossil species consistently found in rock of similar date. Complex life does not occur in the geological record before the oldest, simplest cellular life.

The theory of evolution presupposes an ancient Earth. It concerned Darwin very much that in his time the predominant hypothesis for the age of the Earth was 20 million years. This was simply not a long enough span for evolutionary processes to have produced the diversity of life on Earth. The hypothesis of 20 million years had been put forward by William Thompson (1824–1907), known as Lord Kelvin.

A leading physicist of the 19th century, Kelvin hypothesized that Earth was originally a hot orb created out of a collision of earlier planets and that it had been cooling ever since its formation. Measuring the rate that heat escapes from rocks and the heat at the deepest mine shafts into Earth, Kelvin estimated the Earth's age as no more than 100 million years old. As he added more temperature data, he kept revising his estimate downward, until he came to 20 million years old. What Kelvin did not know was that as

In 1862, William Thompson, known as Lord Kelvin, using a theory of heat flow, calculated that the Earth was 20–40 million years old. This was too old for biblical literalists and too young for geologists and evolutionary biologists.

Earth cooled, new heat also was being generated through radioactivity. When the effects of radioactivity were factored in, scientists calculated that Earth was more than 4 billion years old. This is a more than sufficient time frame for evolution.

Knowledge of radioactivity, which helped scientists date Earth as a whole, also provided a means for dating specific rock layers and fossils. **Isotopic dating** is the name for techniques that measure the amount of radioactive decay in chemicals such as uranium found in rock or in fossilized remains. A variety of measurements based on different isotopes (forms of the same chemical) are now used to cross-check dating estimates and ensure accuracy. These dating procedures have confirmed the evolutionary hypothesis that the simplest forms of fossils will be found in the oldest rocks, while fossils of more complex life, including human life, will come from younger rock.

If, as evolutionary theory predicts, species are related to each other, then it can be predicted that species with similarities should be found close by in time and space. Fish in a particular lake should be more alike to at least some other fish in that same lake region than to fish in similar lakes halfway across the planet. Furthermore, fossils should bear more similarity to living species from their region than to species in similar habitats elsewhere.

The glyptodont, shown in an artist's reconstruction, was about the size of a Volkswagen Beetle, had an armored outer layer, and weighed up to 400 kilograms, about the weight of five men.

©Illustration by: Joe Tucciarone

Examples of this kind were first pointed out by Darwin. He noted that the finches of the Galapagos Island bore resemblance to a finch from the nearest coastline of South America. He also noted that the armadillos of South America bore similarity to fossils of *Glyptodonts*, a much larger armadillo-like creature found on that continent.

Another interesting pattern observed by **biogeographers** (researchers into the distribution and dispersal of species) is termed "local, adaptive radiation." Hawaii has more species of fruit fly than any other location on Earth: one-fourth of the 2,000 species known to exist. The best explanation for this is that the descendants of an early species of fruit fly that made it to the island were able to colonize an open environment, relatively free of competition and predators, and to fill all its niches. The same radiating effects are found for snails and other land mollusks on Hawaii.

Fossil evidence reveals that both porcupines and mountain lions were once numerous in geographic locations where they no longer exist.

In some cases, the habitat of a living species offers no fossil evidence of related species. In such case, evolutionary theory hypothesizes that the ancestral species must have migrated into the territory. And this is what scientists find. A prominent example features the mammals of North and South America. These two continents were separate until the Isthmus of Panama formed some 3 million years ago. Many species found in the South American fossil record now live in North America, and vice versa. The porcupine (originally from South America) and the mountain lion (originally from North America) are just two of the many mammals and plants for which evidence of migration has been found.

Focus of current research

Scientists overwhelmingly accept the concept of "descent with modification" because there is so much evidence in its favor and because it so elegantly and consistently provides an overall framework to explain new discoveries about the biological world. Of many alternatives proposed, not one stands when all the evidence is considered.

Scientists do debate the details, however, and investigation into these issues shows that the theory is so rigorous and so compelling that it attracts inquiry at ever-more sophisticated levels. Here are some of the intriguing questions that propel modern evolutionary inquiry:

• *When did various species first evolve?* Until recently, it was thought that when dinosaurs existed, the only mammals on Earth were as small as mice. Recently, however, paleontologists found the fossil of a weasel-sized mammal with dinosaur bones in its belly — the remains of a meal. The obvious inference is that larger mammals and dinosaurs coexisted. New fossil discoveries like these, new DNA findings, and other pieces of evidence are enabling scientists to create ever-more detailed and accurate "schematic diagrams" that show when species emerged and how they are related to each other.

• *What is a species, anyway?* How does one know whether two organisms are distinct species or merely varieties of the same species? Do two organisms belong to the same species only if they exchange genes in the wild? What if they only mate when they come in contact in captivity? Instead of mating behavior, should species be defined by DNA similarity? Questions about species boundaries may seem arcane to laypeople, but they are important for understanding the processes that drive evolutionary change.

• *What is the pace of evolution?* Charles Darwin proposed that evolution occurs through a steady process of small, incremental steps over great spans of time. But today scientists have proposed that under certain circumstances, evolution may occur much more rapidly. According to one hypothesis, termed **punctuated equilibrium**, a species that has been stable for millions of years evolves into new lineages in a period as brief as a few tens of thousands of years. Such rapid evolution might perhaps be triggered by a major environmental event. Researchers hope that further fossil discoveries as well as laboratory experiments that impose environmental pressure on rapidly generating organisms such as fruit flies may lead to a better understanding of evolution's time frames.

The entwined evolution of insects, birds, and plants, which feed them and which they pollinate, is an example of co-evolution.

• *How much is the evolution of one species related to the evolution of another?* The environment of a population to a large extent determines its evolution. Included in any population's environment are other populations. A key factor in evolution, therefore, may be the interaction between species and between adjacent groups of the

same species. This is called **co-evolution**. In one type of investigation into co-evolution, researchers are looking at whether parasites influence the evolution of their host. For example, they seek to understand how much the malaria virus has affected the evolution of resistance to it in humans. Researchers also are looking at how pairs of species engaged in mutually beneficial relationships influence each other's evolution. How do plants evolve in relationship with the birds and insects that feed from them and pollinate them, and vice versa? How do large fish evolve in relationship with the cleaner shrimp that feed off their bodies, and vice versa? Answers to these kinds of questions about co-evolution may yield insight into other questions, such as why species are so incredibly diverse. It could be that through co-evolution, populations push out in different directions to fill available niches in the environment.

• *How did life originate?* Charles Darwin barely mentioned this question in *The Origin of Species*, because he had no evidence with which to hypothesize. Today, through laboratory research, it may be possible to determine how change can occur from nonliving organic matter to living organisms. Researchers are exploring the ways that organic molecules might, under the right environmental conditions, combine together into proteins and amino acids and then replicate to create living organisms. Working in

Cows pass microorganisms in their saliva and ruminated food to their young. These are necessary for digestion of plant material. Without this transmission, the young calves would likely die. The cow and calves serve as symbiotic hosts for the bacteria. This is another example of co-evolution.

the field of **astrobiology**, scientists are seeking to answer the related question of whether life has occurred only on our planet or also on other planets — put another way, whether life can originate only under a very narrow and unique set of circumstances or within a broader range of physical and chemical processes. Through experiments and through observations of the natural world, scientists are actively seeking to understand the transition to life from non-life. This remains one of the major unsolved challenges in evolution.

FURTHER READING

Benchmarks for Science Literacy, AAAS (Oxford University Press, 1993)

Charles Darwin: Voyaging, Janet Browne (Knopf, 1995)

Charles Darwin: The power of place, E. Janet Browne (Princeton University Press, 2003)

Evolution: The remarkable history of a scientific theory, Edward J. Larson (Modern Library, 2004)

The Growth of Biological Thought: Diversity, evolution, and inheritance, Ernst Mayr (Belknap Press, 1985)

On the Origin of Species, Charles Darwin (IndyPublish.com, 2002)

Science for All Americans, F. James Rutherford and Andrew Ahlgren; AAAS (Oxford University Press, 1990)

Initial responses to Darwin's theory

Angela Rawlett knocked on the open door of Phil Compton's office in the campus ministry building. "Hello," she said to the man inside. "Am I disturbing you?"

"Angela!" Phil responded as he looked up from the journal he was reading, which Angela saw was in some language other than English. "Will you have coffee with me again?" Phil stood up from his desk and walked over to a credenza where his coffeemaker was set up. Angela stepped inside his office and perched on the edge of the armchair near the door.

"Actually, I just picked up a drink," she said, taking a juice bottle out of her backpack. "I want to thank you for helping me decide to stick with my biology major. The evolution class is certainly, umm, *interesting*, and I can handle it, I think. But I have been wondering why evolution is so cruel. It's a horribly designed system, don't you think?"

"Whether you credit evolution or not, the lion kills the antelope," said the religious advisor.

Angela opened her mouth as if to reply but said nothing.

"Besides, there's horror everywhere you look," answered Phil as he carried a china cup over to his armchair and sat down. "Not just in the competition for survival. Earthquakes. Forest fires."

"Hatred," added Angela, sliding into her chair. "Human arrogance and corruption."

"Yes, you understand. We could go on forever. Nonetheless, the question you raise about evolution is valid. It is an issue of theodicy."

"I haven't learned that term in my biology class yet."

"It's not a scientific term," answered Phil. "It is a theological term. Theodicy: God and justice. It refers to efforts to understand how God can be good and almighty though there is evil in the world."

"I can see how God might want to create a lot of variety, you know, like the thousands of forms of plants," explained Angela. "But I find it hard to believe that God would have to resort to such a destructive system to create all that life."

"It's an interesting conundrum, and an old one, but it's not for science to solve," answered Phil as he removed his glasses, polished them on the end of his tie, and put them back on again. "It may comfort you to know that many scientists who fully accept the theory of evolution have been Christians. Even the great Charles Darwin himself believed in God, though he did struggle with aspects of faith."

"Yes, I know," answered Angela. "The Ichneumon wasp."

Phil looked puzzled until he recognized her reference. "Ah yes. The wasp that lays its eggs inside living caterpillars. Darwin had trouble conceiving of a God that could create a creature such as that. But before we get too depressed about the horrors of this world, I want to make sure you know that some Christians in Darwin's time who opposed the theory of evolution did so not because of this problem of evil, but rather, on scientific grounds."

Samuel Wilberforce, Bishop of Oxford.

"What do you mean?" asked the student.

"Has your evolution class by chance discussed the legendary encounter between Samuel Wilberforce, Bishop of Oxford, and Thomas Henry Huxley?" Angela shook her head no. "It took place in 1860, the year after *The Origin of Species* was published, at a meeting of a British scientific association," Phil explained. "Wilberforce presented a critique of evolution. At his conclusion, he supposedly made the mistake of teasing Huxley, a staunch Darwin defender, by asking whether he was descended on his grandmother's or grandfather's side from an ape."

Angela smiled. "How did Huxley respond?"

"He one-upped the bishop. He basically said that given the choice of being descended from a foolish windbag or an ape, he would prefer the latter."

"Ouch."

"Historians now think this anecdote is inaccurate, though the incident is often portrayed as the

Evolution Dialogues

great victory of the evolutionary argument over the religious," Phil continued. "But the fact is, Wilberforce was attending that meeting not merely as a protestor but as a participant in science. Darwin admitted that the bishop's critique of *Origins* was uncommonly clever and targeted its weakest points. The bishop himself said that he would not back away from any facts merely because they appeared to contradict what is in the Bible. He simply felt that Darwin's evidence for evolution was insufficient."

"Was it?" asked Angela.

"Darwin and his contemporaries did not know about the genetic mechanisms upon which natural selection works," Phil responded. "And in Darwin's time, few fossils of transitional forms had been found to support his ideas about the branching evolution of species."

"I'm sorry. I'm not following your point," Angela said. "Are you trying to say that evolution is scientifically weak?"

Thomas Henry Huxley.

©The British Library

"Not at all," Phil responded. "I'm saying that there is nothing inherent in evolution that is antagonistic to Christian belief. In fact, for many Christians, evolution has enriched their conception of God. I'm not being flippant when I say that evolutionary science has helped me envision God as the leader of a cosmic jazz session."

Phil lifted his cup to take another sip, saw that it was empty, and set it down. "And among scientists, you will find Christians, including Evangelical Christians, along with scientists of other persuasions, who have endorsed Darwin's original theory of evolution *and* who have pointed out problems and gaps that need to be resolved. Scientists of all stripes have refined the theory through further discovery and research. But there is no *ipso facto* conflict."

"Yet there is conflict," Angela persisted.

"Yes. We humans always seem to find ways to argue."

"And there is mystery, too."

"Mystery?" asked the cleric.

"The mystery of motivation," the student responded as she tossed her empty juice bottle into a wastebasket by the chair. "God's motivation. I still would like to understand that."

CHAPTER 4

Initial responses to Darwin's theory

Photograph by Julia Margaret Cameron. ©Wellcome Library, London

During Darwin's lifetime, six editions of the *Origins* were published, involving 35 printings and translations in 11 languages.

A topic of personal interest

When Charles Darwin (1809–1882) published *On the Origin of Species* in 1859, the entire print run of 1,250 copies was sold out in the first day. Before he died 23 years later, five more editions had been produced in England, for a total of more than 12,000 copies, plus various editions in Germany, France, the United States, and other countries. For a book on a scientific topic in the 19th century, this was a major success.

There are several ways to explain the interest in Darwin's book. For the upper class as well as the educated middle class that was emerging in the mid-1800s, one was expected to keep current on cultural happenings, including events in the sciences. It helped that Darwin had aimed his book at the general reader and wrote in elegant, readable prose.

Furthermore, interest had been primed for such a work by the rising number of scientific books, periodicals, and lectures available for public consumption. In particular, the 1844, publication of *Vestiges of the Natural History of Creation* was a watershed event that made the evolution controversy a common topic of parlor conversation. *Vestiges* was authored anonymously by Robert Chambers (1802–1871), an Edinburgh publisher with a keen interest in natural history but no particular training in it. Though his scientific arguments were ill informed, his writing style was captivating, and his book popularized the notion of a natural yet God-ordained progression to history.

Perhaps the greatest reason that people clamored to read about Darwin's theory was because they recognized that it affected them personally. *The Origin of Species* took humankind off its pinnacle as the ultimate purpose of God's creation and placed it on the meandering path of evolution. This shook the Victorian self-image to its very core. Other cherished beliefs were in the balance as well, such as humankind's special relationship to God. Evolution raised the question of whether morality itself stemmed from that relationship with God or was merely an evolved behavior helpful to survival.

AGITATED TAILOR (to foreign-looking gentleman), *"Y-you're rather l-long in the arm, S-sir, b-b-but I'll d-d-do my b-b-best to fit you!"*

©Wellcome Library, London; Punch, 28 December 1861

The "monkey-to-man" question — to use a grossly inaccurate but popular phrase of the time — was both profound and titillating, making for great copy and conversation. Spurred by riveting questions of identity and meaning, the public argued about Darwinian evolution in their clubs and pubs and dinner parties; debated it at meetings of scientific societies; wrote about it endlessly in newspapers, magazines, review journals, and private correspondence; and preached on it from church pulpits.

Rejection

The first review of *The Origin of Species* was scathing. The anonymous author (reviews were often anonymous in those days) wrote: "If a monkey has become a man — what may not a man become?"[12] The reviewer declared the book dangerous.

Similar concern also prevented Darwin from receiving the support of an old mentor. Adam Sedgwick (1785–1873), professor of geology at Cambridge University, did not have any problem with the proposition that change had occurred to the Earth and its species over eons of time. However, he ardently believed that such change was designed and driven by a divine creator, and he didn't like it that Darwin's theory did not explicitly say so. He was upset by Darwin's proposal that evolution worked through natural selection, a seemingly mechanical and purposeless scheme that did not take a creator into account.

"There is a moral or metaphysical part of nature as well as a physical," he wrote to Darwin after reading the copy his former protégé sent to him. "...Tis the crown & glory of organic science that it *does* thro' final cause, link material to moral."[13] **"Final Cause"** and **"First Cause"** are classical phrases used to refer to the ultimate hand behind earthly events. By not crediting evolution to a divine initiator, Sedgwick felt that Darwin divorced humanity from its reason for being and so degraded it. Sedgwick implored Darwin to embrace God's revelation and implied that he would be denied the afterlife if he did not.

Another former ally turned against him. Richard Owen (1804–1892), superintendent of the natural history collections at the British Museum, once had done Darwin a good turn by analyzing the fossil and animal specimens Darwin and the crew of the HMS Beagle had brought back from the Galapagos Islands. Yet Owen was harshly critical of Darwin's new theory, in part because it competed with his own explanation for the similarity between species (this was the idea that God worked from **archetypes,** or basic structural plans that were adapted to each different species). Owen argued that Darwin's theory lacked sufficient evidence. Like Sedgwick, Owen felt Darwin was wrongly divorcing science from its appropriate role, which was to illuminate God's work.

Samuel Wilberforce (1805–1873), Bishop of Oxford, was a prominent opponent of Darwin's theory. Wilberforce delighted in conflict — his nickname was "Soapy Sam" for his slippery arguments. Back in 1844, when Robert Chambers had published his evolutionary ideas in *Vestiges of the Natural History of Creation,* Wilberforce had been a vocal critic against them. Once Darwin's book was published, the bishop quickly aimed his powerful speaking and writing skills against the new theory.

Within the Roman Catholic Church, one of the first responses came from the German

Richard Owen, super-intendent of the natural history collections at the British Museum

©The British Library

Catholic bishops. They issued a condemnation of the idea of natural human evolution, stating that it was "clearly opposed to Sacred Scripture and to the Faith."[14]

Ironically, Darwin also failed to gain the support of Robert FitzRoy (1805–1865), the man who had captained the Beagle when Darwin was aboard ship. FitzRoy made his own lasting contributions to science through his efforts to establish methods of weather prediction as a means of improving the lives of seafarers. He was a zealous advocate for Christianity who attempted to bring his religious faith to the people he met on his round-the-world travels. FitzRoy spoke out against Darwin's theory of evolution, because it conflicted with a literal understanding of the Genesis account of creation. He found degrading the proposition that humanity descended from ape-like ancestors.

One of Darwin's most vocal scientific opponents in North America was Harvard paleontologist Louis Agassiz.

Over in America, Darwin's ideas were met with strong opposition from Louis Agassiz (1807–1873), a highly respected naturalist at Harvard University. Agassiz had literally been a student of Georges Cuvier (1769–1832) and, like his teacher, he favored the hypothesis that changes to the Earth and its creatures had been caused by sudden, cataclysmic events and other unique processes no longer in operation. Agassiz was unsympathetic to Darwin's evolutionary theory on scientific grounds; he was not convinced by the data available in his day. He also had philosophical though not specifically biblical objections. Evolutionary theory contradicted his view of nature as one grand and interconnected unity. Furthermore, evolution and its implications of species change did not fit into Agassiz's understanding of nature as fixed and perfectly balanced according to a divine plan. It was one of his personal disappointments that by his death virtually all of his students had adopted evolutionary views of one sort or another.

Qualified acceptance

Darwin himself was disappointed by the equivocation of certain learned people whose opinions he highly respected. First among these was Charles Lyell (1797–1875), whose theory of geological change over time had so influenced Darwin. Lyell gave Darwin tremendous personal support both before

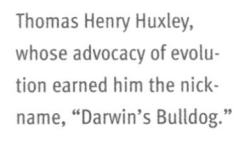

Alfred Russel Wallace, the co-originator of the theory of evolution by means of natural selection.

and after publication of his theory. However, there were aspects of Darwin's theory that Lyell found difficult to reconcile with his beliefs about humankind's special position in God's creation.

Lyell acknowledged that Darwin's theory was able to account for many of the facts he himself had helped uncover about humanity's antique lineage. Lyell had helped demonstrate that the Earth had existed long enough to allow for humans to have evolved from a common ancestor with apes. And yet he rejected the idea that *Homo sapiens* also had evolved. The observable distance between the features of contemporary apes and humans indicated to Lyell that humankind had acquired reason through some single leap (the first pre-human fossils had only just been discovered and Lyell did not have them for consideration). He preferred to allow this question to remain a mystery without rational explanation.

Darwin could not even claim the unqualified endorsement of Alfred Russel Wallace (1823–1913), the co-originator of the theory of evolution through the means of natural selection. The two had an amiable relationship, and after the publication of Darwin's *The Origin of Species*, they continued to correspond about evolution theory. Nonetheless, Wallace asserted that natural selection did not apply to humans.

Thomas Henry Huxley, whose advocacy of evolution earned him the nickname, "Darwin's Bulldog."

Enthusiastic support

The most ardent promoter of the theory of evolution was Darwin's friend Thomas Henry Huxley (1825–1895). A lecturer at the School of Mines in London, Huxley was a biologist who did groundbreaking research in zoology and paleontology. He is famously known to have remarked immediately after reading *The Origin of Species*, "How extremely stupid not to have thought of that!"[15]

Huxley was candid to Darwin and the public about certain problems he had with the theory, particularly with the details of how natural selection might work. Huxley also believed that modern humans because of their ethics and intellect were

no longer subject to evolutionary forces. Yet in a note to Darwin shortly after the book appeared, Huxley wrote that he was eager to defend it and described the "claws" and "beaks" he was "sharpening" in readiness for debate.[16] Huxley launched into a whirlwind of lectures and reviews to propound and defend the theory of evolution. For this he earned the nickname "Darwin's Bulldog."

Huxley coined the term **agnostic** to describe himself as someone who thought that the question of God's existence was unanswerable. He did not claim to be an **atheist**, that is, he refused to deny the existence of God. Rather, he favored an approach to understanding the world that was based on evidence from nature itself.

Another important and loyal promoter of Darwin's theory was Joseph Hooker (1814–1879), a botanist who eventually assumed the position of director of Britain's Royal Botanic Gardens at Kew, an important center for botanical research. The two had become friends after Darwin asked Hooker to classify the plants he had brought back from the Galapagos Islands. Hooker was the first colleague in whom Darwin confided, in correspondence, that he had developed a theory of evolution by natural selection. Over years of correspondence, Hooker gave advice, critiqued Darwin's arguments, and helped garner botanical evidence for natural selection.

After publication of *The Origin of Species,* Hooker was a behind-the-scenes supporter, arranging for the publication of reviews, encouraging its discussion by scientific societies in Britain's many colonies around the world, and helping explain the theory to fence-sitting colleagues. Through his influential position at Kew, he continued to promote botanical research that documented natural selection. Hooker was a churchgoer. At the same time, his sympathies were with the reason-based worldview of Huxley.

Plant samples that Darwin colleted from the Galapagos Islands offered botanical evidence for natural selection.

An early and important endorsement from the Christian community came from the Reverend Charles Kingsley (1819–1875), who was respected throughout England as a serious intellectual because he had published many pamphlets and novels advocating reform such as improvement of conditions for the working poor. He also was chaplain to Queen Victoria. After reading Darwin's book, Kingsley wrote to the author: "All that I have seen of it awes me. Both with the heap of facts, & the prestige of your name, & also with the clear intuition, that if you be right, I must give up much that I have believed & written."[17]

Kingsley was open to scientifically revealed information, believing it could shed light on his religious understanding. At the same time, he felt that scientists should be open to religious revelation because it would enhance their intellectual understanding of the world. Kingsley conceived of a God in all of nature, not just in its beautiful and beneficial aspects. He did not see a conflict between belief in a God who created the world and belief in a God who worked through evolutionary processes to do so. He wrote Darwin that he believed it could be just as noble for God to work in this way as to intervene directly. Darwin considered Kingsley's endorsement so important that he included the clergyman's letter in subsequent editions of his book.

Another important early endorsement from the Christian community came from the Reverend Baden Powell (1796–1860), father of the founder of the scouting movement, professor of geometry at Oxford University, and a contributor to a controversial volume of essays by theologians with liberal approaches to biblical interpretation. This volume, called *Essays and Reviews,* was published just a few months after Darwin's book. In it, Powell wrote that Darwin's theory "must soon bring about an entire revolution of opinion in favor of the grand principle of the self-evolving powers of nature."[18]

Across the Atlantic, Darwin had another important supporter in the figure of Asa Gray (1818–1888), a professor of natural history at Harvard University and America's leading botanist and a Presbyterian. Darwin corresponded with Gray prior to publication for help in refining his ideas. After publication, they sustained a long and cordial correspondence about various aspects of the theory and its meaning. Gray wrote several positive reviews that appeared in North American publications and he arranged for the American edition of *The Origin of Species.*

Gray had opposed evolutionary theories that had been proposed earlier. While he was convinced by Darwin's arguments, he had some difficulty with the concept of natural selection. Gray was able to assimilate the scientific

Evolution Dialogues

theory through an understanding of it that has come to be called **theistic evolution** — the assumption that God influences the process of evolution.

Evolution of scientific and public opinion

There were a great many other prominent personalities who weighed in publicly on Darwin's theory when it was first presented. Indeed, the ones just described merely represent the range of voices that were heard. A wide variety of views were expressed on both the theory as a whole and over certain aspects of it such as natural selection and human evolution but most of all over its implications.

Yet within a few years after *The Origin of Species* appeared, opinions sorted into two camps. Thomas Huxley was the unofficial leader of the pro-Darwin forces, while Bishop Wilberforce and Richard Owen rallied the cause against the new theory. In America, Asa Gray threw his weight behind the theory and Louis Agassiz against it. Many of the public figures debating the theory of evolution had forceful personalities, powerful positions, career rivalries, personal agendas, and strongly held philosophical or religious convictions. This exacerbated the differences they perceived themselves to have over the theory itself. Others were forced in effect to choose sides.

Despite the public controversy, scientists quickly began to examine Darwin's evidence and add their own findings to it. A main concern was whether the Earth was old enough to accommodate evolutionary history. Another concern had to do with the many gaps in the fossil record. Such concerns were eventually overcome by new evidence from the fields of geology

A main concern about Darwin's theory was whether the Earth was old enough to accommodate evolutionary history.

and paleontology. Within the quick span of about 15 years, the vast majority of scientists came to accept evolution as a credible and useful theory that explained the facts and allowed for the prediction and testing of a wide variety of hypotheses about life on Earth.

Darwin's mechanism of natural selection did not achieve full scientific acceptance until well into the 20th century. This delay stemmed from the problem of heredity. In Darwin's time, it was hypothesized that traits of parents blended in their children. This was problematic for natural selection because it meant that favorable traits that emerged through mutation would be diluted in succeeding generations. Genetic discoveries eventually helped reveal the hereditary principles that could allow new, useful traits to persevere in a species.

Among the general public, once the hubbub died down, there was little resistance to the common-sense premise that change occurs over time. Given the geological evidence, most people also did not have trouble accepting the lengthy timeline for Earth's history assumed by evolution. Many even found reasonable the scientific explanations for how plants and animals evolved. Many had no difficulty with the concept that humans emerged through evolution as well.

Even the mechanism of natural selection was not publicly controversial though some scientists remained unconvinced until genetic processes were discovered that made it plausible. Some historians credit this to the fact that most members of the public did not really understand natural selection and so ignored that part of the theory or simply assumed that God actively made the selections. But perhaps a more significant reason why the general public accepted natural selection was because it could be used to justify a variety of nonscientific and even contradictory views about society.

According to one such perspective, some individuals or groups have advantage over others because of their innate biological and moral superiority. Progress will occur if they are allowed to prevail naturally and without interference; thus, it is futile to interfere with the winnowing effects of evolution. An entirely different perspective combined natural selection with the older theory of Jean-Baptiste Lamarck (1744–1829), which proposed that traits acquired in an individual's lifetime could be incorporated into the species. According to this viewpoint, traits conducive to success could be found at *any* level of society and *anyone* could acquire fitness and thrive through individual initiative and effort.

A third viewpoint held that humans had acquired through evolution the intelligence to influence their future evolution and so move the species even

Industrialists of the late 19th and early 20th centuries, like Andrew Carnegie, often assumed a "survival of the fittest" economic philosophy and also were philanthropists, who funded libraries and universities as institutions to support individuals striving for self-improvement.

further toward perfection. This perspective was used to impose a variety of social selection efforts such as intelligence testing, immigration quotas, sterilization laws, and enforced segregation. A converse reading of evolution was that humans had acquired cooperative and altruistic behaviors through the process of nature; therefore, group effort and benevolent interventions that uplifted the weak could in fact advance humanity. The terms **Social Evolutionism** and **Social Darwinism** have been used by historians to describe these various social analogies drawn from the science.

The English philosopher Herbert Spencer (1820–1903), who coined the phrase "survival of the fittest," advocated for a free market and limited intervention from governments or workers' unions. Of like mind was William Graham Sumner (1840–1910), professor of political economy at Yale University and a former Episcopal minister. Spencer and Sumner argued against laws intended to extend assistance to the poor or to provide government-sponsored education. Andrew Carnegie (1835–1919) and other industrialists of the era benefited from the laissez faire philosophy that flowed readily from "survival of the fittest" ideology. Yet at the same time, these so-called robber barons were leading philanthropists who funded libraries and universities and other institutions that allowed for individual self-improvement. The Englishman Francis Galton (1822–1911), a cousin of Darwin and an eminent scientist in his own right, coined the term **eugenics** to describe policies he advocated for keeping advanced humans free from the degenerating influence of the less evolved. American progressives such as Jane Addams (1860–1935) and Samuel Gompers (1850–1924) worked with the poor to improve their selective social environments, that is, their living and working conditions, and advocated for their rights. In their disparate ways, all of these people were influenced by the social application of Darwinian ideas.

Evolving Christian responses

Evolutionary theory's endorsement by the scientific community stimulated some religious thinkers to come to terms with the theory themselves by considering evolution as an instrument of God. This religious development was helped along by the fact that many influential scientists endorsing evolutionary theory also believed in God and belonged to churches. For the many lay Christians who did not hold themselves to a strict and literal reading of the Bible, evolution quickly sorted out as a non-issue. For such Christians, the purpose of the Bible was to reveal the lessons of God through words and stories that could be universally understood; they did not hold to it as a textbook of science and so they did not find in biblical language contradictions to the science of evolution.

The Roman Catholic Church in the late 19th century wrestled with the challenge that contemporary science put to its traditional interpretations of the Bible. In his 1893 encyclical *Providentissimus Deus* ("On the Study of Holy Scripture"), Pope Leo XIII (1810–1903) addressed the dynamic between biblical scholars and scientists. "There can never, indeed, be any real discrepancy between the theologian and the physicist, as long as each confines himself within his own lines, and both are careful, as St. Augustine warns us, 'not to make rash assertions, or to assert what is not known as known.'" The Pope defended the inerrancy of the Bible, but he also noted that church theologians both ancient and modern are not inerrant, "for it may be that, in commenting on passages where physical matters occur, they have sometimes expressed the ideas of their own times, and thus made statements which in these days have been abandoned as incorrect."

Into the first part of the 20th century, the Vatican did not issue any direct pronouncements on Darwin's theory, but it did place some works by Catholic authors defending human evolution on its Index of Forbidden Books. Father John Zahm (1851–1921) was a Holy Cross Father at Notre Dame. His 1898 book *Evolution and Dogma* sought to show the compatibility of evolution with Christian teaching. It missed being placed on the List of Forbidden Books only because he withdrew all copies from sale. All the while, Catholic intel-

In the late 19th century, Pope Leo XIII affirmed that the Bible was inerrant but that theologians were not, so that some earlier interpretations of scripture could be erroneous in the light of new scientific knowledge.

PAVLVS·V·BVRGHESIVS·ROMANVS·PONTMA

lectuals engaged in thoughtful theological debate. Ultimately, the issue centered on the status of human beings. Eventually a consensus emerged within Roman Catholicism that the human soul was "infused" directly by God, but the human body may have evolved from animal predecessors.

In the United States, Catholic response was complicated by contemporary events. Some social activists opposed to the influx of European Catholic immigrants argued that such people were unfit and would degrade the American race. This eugenic argument was a social not a scientific claim, and in fact it grossly distorted the science. Nonetheless, many Catholics offended by eugenics also rejected evolution. At the same time, progressive Catholics in the United States were embracing new ideals not held by the church's leadership back in Rome, such as individual liberty and separation of church and state. When these progressive Catholics also saw merit in evolutionary theory, this furthered the official church's resistance to it.

In the United States, Catholic response to evolution was complicated by other contemporary events including increased Catholic immigration from Europe and the rise of the eugenics movement.

In the United States, there was no resistance to evolution organized by the **mainline denominations**. These are the older branches of various Protestant denominations from which newer denominations broke off at one time or another in the 19th century and beyond. They include the Episcopal Church, the American Baptist Church, the United Methodist Church, the Presbyterian Church (USA), the Evangelical Lutheran Church, and the United Church of Christ.

Even some **evangelical Christians** respectfully received evolutionary theory. The term "evangelical" is derived from the Greek word for "good news" or "gospel," which is the message of the Bible's New Testament. Evangelicalism is a form of Christianity that puts emphasis on one's personal experience and faith, the importance of being "reborn" in Jesus Christ, and proselytizing outreach to "nonbelievers." For some evangelicals, the Bible was understood to reveal both the past and the future without error and so was not open to other than literal interpretation. Some evangelical ideas, such as that Jesus was personally involved in each person's life, were difficult to square with evolutionary theory. Nonetheless, members of this community engaged each other on the topic in collegial dialogue.

In fact, a good number of the leading evangelical thinkers of the early 20th century expressed ideas about how evolution could be accommodated to their doctrinal positions, and some even drew from the theory to expand their theological perspectives. A representative member of this community was B. B. Warfield (1851–1921), a biblical scholar and professor at Princeton Theological Seminary who wrote one of the seminal essays on **biblical inerrancy**. In his various writings on evolutionary theory, Warfield explored the points of convergence and divergence. He took issue with the description of natural selection as an uncontrolled process, arguing that such a statement was not science but rather "a philosophy of the universe." To Warfield, evolutionary processes occurred through natural laws, which were the expression of God's will. Warfield acknowledged that the theory had earned credibility from scientists even as they debated the details, and so he sought to keep an open mind.

The response from other religions

The anxiety that Darwin's theory provoked within Christianity stands in contrast to its relatively placid reception by other major faiths. Neither Judaism, Islam, nor the major Asian religions were perturbed by its introduction.

Judaism by tradition reads its holy scriptures through *midrash*, a process of interpretation and commentary by religious scholars. Over the centuries, many volumes of interpretation have been published and have been incorporated into the tradition. As part of *midrash*, Jewish scholars have interpreted scripture using the science of their time. For most people of the Jewish faith, evolution was readily adopted as a context in which to interpret the Genesis creation story.

Islam's holy book, the Koran, contains a great many references to the natural world, which is therefore considered real, important, and good. Given such a perspective, the study of nature flourished in early Islam, during the Dark Ages of Europe. Later, however, Islam was influenced by skepticism as to whether God and God's creation could be known or described at all. Scientific and theological speculation was disdained as self-indulgent and unprovable. Thus, when Darwin's theory of evolution first emerged, it did not register significantly within Islam. Furthermore, to Muslims, the Koran is God's word. Since human comprehension of that word is limited, there is always new opportunity to understand its meaning. As a consequence, some Muslim scholars identify contemporary scientific discoveries to have been already present in the Koran as read today. However, Muslims do object to interpretations of evolution that are materialist and reductionist, that is, that eliminate all possibility of a God-driven world.

Asian religious traditions such as Buddhism, Confucianism, and Daoism are non-monotheistic, which means they do not assume an all-powerful creator god who dispenses mercy and judgment. Creation accounts are incidental elements of these traditions. As a result, Darwin's theory did not challenge any parallel creation narratives the way it did with Christianity and it did not raise up questions concerning the role of a god in the world.

In some respects, the Asian religions align well with evolutionary theory. For example, in the Hindu religion, life is an endless cycle of creation and destruction. Into this, the long timeline of "descent with modification" can easily be read. In the Buddhist tradition, the idea that *Homo sapiens* are a species created over billions of years of evolution dovetails with the Buddhist idea that humans are enslaved by mental delusions. Such delusions can be thought of as adaptive mechanisms that allowed humans to make their way in their environments, but with a cost.

Judaism, Islam, and the major Asian religions have responded differently than Christianity to the theory of evolution.

Buildup toward a backlash

Scientific opinion had coalesced in support of evolution by the early decades of the 20th century, and the theory was taught in most biology textbooks at both the high school and college levels. Then several factors converged to create a backlash.

One such factor was the rise of **fundamentalist Christianity**. This off-shoot movement of evangelical Christianity received its name from a series of little pamphlets, "The Fundamentals: A Testimony to the Truth," that were published between the years 1910 and 1915. Wealthy patrons of a Bible institute in Los Angeles underwrote the costs of publication. They also paid for the costs of distributing the pamphlets free of charge to every pastor, professor, and theology student in the country.

"The Fundamentals" reasserted certain truths that had been called into question by scholars who, using the methods of higher criticism, challenged traditional views of the authorship and meaning of the books of the Bible. These were the truths that, according to the booklet series, were undisputable:

- The Bible is true and free from error (at least in the versions of Scripture God inspired in the original authors).
- Christ was born of a virgin woman, Mary.
- Jesus Christ atoned for human sin by dying on the cross.
- Jesus came back to life, in his own body, after his death.
- Jesus performed miracles.

Each booklet contained several essays. A number of those essays addressed evolution, but their authors did not all take the same position. For

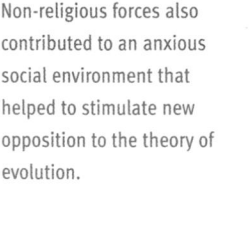
©William H. Rau, Library of Congress

example, some accepted the idea of evolution as the means by which God creates, some rejected evolution altogether, and some accepted animal evolution but rejected human evolution. The main thrust of "The Fundamentals," however, was that the story of creation as described in the Bible was the correct version and that God has been directly involved in all earthly goings-on.

Non-religious forces also contributed to an anxious social environment that helped to stimulate new opposition to the theory of evolution.

©Library of Congress

©Library of Congress

Other, non-religious forces were also at work to create a backlash against the theory of evolution. In the United States, these included the rise of industrialism, the trauma created by the Civil War and its aftermath, the great influx of Jewish and Catholic (that is, non-Protestant) immigrants, and contentious arguments over alcohol, women's suffrage, and the rights of formerly enslaved people. People were threatened by change and insecurity, and this made it more difficult for them to consider a theory in which change and contingency were central.

Another factor contributing to the backlash against evolution was the social application of Darwinism as espoused by Spencer and Sumner, which compromised the Christian ethics of compassion and justice. Many people were repulsed by the excesses of unfettered capitalism, the suppression of labor unions, and governmental disregard for the needs of the poor. Such people tended to also reject the science that had been appropriated to defend such social practices.

Evolutionary theory also suffered from its association with Germany, a problematic connection on several counts. Higher criticism had emerged out of that country, and some Christians were offended by this opening of a door to a naturalistic explanation of Scripture. The hideous carnage of World War I, in which Germany was a major antagonist, gave rise to disgust in human-centered enterprises and a desire by some Christians to reassert God's authority.

Probably the specific factor that triggered the backlash against evolution in the United States was the rapid increase in the number of children receiving public secondary school education. For most Americans before the turn of the century, the teaching of evolution was a non-issue because their children did not stay in school long enough to learn anything about it. As universal education spread across the United States, the numbers of pupils at all levels of public schooling increased rapidly. What children were being taught about evolution became a real concern for parents who were sympathetic to fundamentalism, opposed to "survival of the fittest" social policies, or both.

A rapidly increasing population of publicly educated schoolchildren following the turn of the 20th century also contributed to a public reaction against teaching evolution.

William Jennings Bryan (seated at left) being interrogated by Clarence Seward Darrow, during the trial of State of Tennessee vs. John Thomas Scopes, July 20, 1925.

Evolution on trial

By the 1920s, activists were lobbying against the teaching of evolution in public schools. The first law to criminalize the teaching of evolution was adopted in 1925 by Tennessee. This set off a course of events often identified in history books as the **Scopes Monkey Trial**. The American Civil Liberties Union (ACLU) wanted to challenge Tennessee's anti-evolution law and so announced that it would defend any teacher in the state who dared to break it. Civic leaders in the small town of Dayton thought that a trial might bring some good publicity, so they found a teacher willing to take up the ACLU's challenge. John Scopes (1900–1970) had briefly taught from a text that included lessons about evolution while serving as a substitute biology teacher.

At the ensuing trial, the prosecution team included William Jennings Bryan (1860–1925), a three-time contender for president, a social progressive, and a Christian who had been spearheading a campaign against the teaching of evolution mainly for what he felt were its corroding effects on the human soul and society. Joining the ACLU on the defense was Clarence Darrow (1857–1938), a high-profile criminal defense attorney. Darrow was an agnostic who was not sympathetic to traditional religion. With these two celebrities pitted against each other, the trial became a national sensation. It was the first court proceeding to be broadcast on radio, and America was captivated by it.

In the end, Scopes was found guilty and fined $100, but the case was later dismissed by the Tennessee Supreme Court on a technicality. What is most remembered about the Scopes trial today is the supposed humiliation dealt to Bryan when Darrow goaded him into appearing on the witness stand

Evolution Dialogues

to defend the biblical account of creation. The court record suggests that Bryan held his own in the face of Darrow's examination. However, the popular memory has been shaped more by the depiction of the event in a later play, *Inherit the Wind*, than by the actual historical record. In fact, the anti-evolution forces were not undone. The Tennessee law forbidding the teaching of human evolution stayed on the books for more than 40 years, and four other states passed anti-evolution laws before the end of the decade. An even greater number were proposed but defeated.

The fundamentalists, working through local school boards, were successful in suppressing the teaching of human evolution in any number of school districts. Even more significantly, by mid-century, the subject of evolution had dropped almost entirely out of textbooks — and out of the public conversation.

In the first hundred years after it was proposed by Darwin, the theory of evolution gained considerable scientific credibility. It also earned widespread public acceptance for discrete ideas such as that the Earth is very old and change occurs over time within and even through lineages of species. Many people who held Christian beliefs were able to make the transition to the new scientific worldview without abandoning their religious convictions, often by compartmentalizing each. Yet evolutionary theory did open up a veritable can of worms with respect to its religious implications. In a world affected by evolution, what is God's role and what is humankind's place? These questions were very challenging and, for many, it was easier to bury the theory than to face it.

FURTHER READING

The Post-Darwinian Controversies: A study of the Protestant struggle to come to terms with Darwin in Great Britain and America, 1870–1900, James R. Moore (Cambridge University Press, 1981)

Darwin's Forgotten Defenders: The encounter between evangelical theology and evolutionary thought, David N. Livingstone (Regent College Publishing, 1984)

God and Nature: Historical essays on the encounter between Christianity and science, David C. Lindberg and Ronald L. Numbers, eds. (University of California Press, 1986)

Summer for the Gods: The Scopes trial and America's continuing debate over science and religion, Edward J. Larson (Harvard University Press, 1998)

When Science and Christianity Meet, David C. Lindberg and Ronald L. Numbers, eds. (University of California Press, 2003)

The science behind evolution

Angela Rawlett rapped lightly on the door to the office of her advisor, Laurel Dunbar. "Hi," the student said. "Can I come — *Whoa!* What is that?" She stared at the computer screen on her advisor's desk.

Dr. Dunbar looked up from the papers before her and followed the student's gaze to the vibrant floral images floating in and out of focus. "My orchids," she said, smiling. "Aren't they gorgeous? I could gaze at them forever."

"Your orchids?"

"I don't actually own all these flowers," said the advisor as she waved Angela toward a chair. "Some pose for me, others I go hunting for. I use a single-lens reflex camera — digital of course — using a macro lens and a ring flash. Do you do photography?"

"No," said Angela. "But I could show you some beautiful catalogs of tomatoes."

"I'll bet you could," said Dr. Dunbar. "My neighbor raises beautiful heirloom varieties. She had some exotic ones last summer — especially the Marizol Purple. What brings you by?"

Angela pulled her gaze away from the shifting monitor images. "I got in an argument with my dad last weekend that really has me stumped."

"I love a story."

"He was on the phone negotiating stud fees," the student continued. "After he hung up, we got talking about animal breeding. Before I knew it, we were in an argument about evolution."

"Fascinating," said Dr. Dunbar, leaning back in her chair. "I love a good argument."

"My dad says it's one thing to improve a line of cattle through selective breeding, but that cows evolving through other species is impossible," Angela explained. "And then he said that evolution is just a theory anyway; it's not a fact. And then I didn't know what to say."

"Why not?"

"Because in my biology class, Dr. Brown does refer to evolution as a theory. So my dad was right. But Dr. Brown also talked about how new species are formed through macroevolution. So my dad was wrong. Except, how do we know anything for sure about evolution, if it's just a theory?"

Dr. Dunbar started to say something but Angela interrupted her. "Look," the young woman said. "Before you get the wrong impression, I want you to know that my dad is a pretty cool guy. He's smart, and I really respect his opinion, even though we had this fight."

Dr. Dunbar tapped her fingertips together and gazed thoughtfully at them. "You say your dad is cool," she said. "Is he really cool? I mean, if we took his temperature, would it read 38.6 instead of 98.6?"

"Of course not," Angela said. "That's not what I meant."

"Precisely — or rather, imprecisely," responded the professor with a sly grin. "Sometimes we use a word differently in different contexts. And so I might say in casual conversation that I have a theory about why fathers and daughters get into arguments, but I would be referring to some hunch of mine. But in science when we talk about a theory, we mean an overarching explanatory framework that has been carefully constructed. A scientific theory is based on facts that have been gathered through observation and it has been tested under a variety of hypotheses."

"But if facts are true, aren't theories based on facts true, too?"

"Sometimes what we accept as facts are later discovered to be wrong — but more important to your question, a theory can be

Evolution Dialogues

refined or strengthened by the discovery of new facts. In some cases, it can even be overturned. But it can never be proven definitively, because there are an infinite number of new facts yet to be discovered that may offer us a better perspective. Nonetheless, a well-grounded theory does point toward the truth."

Angela thought for a moment. "If I can't say the theory of evolution is true, then I don't know how to answer my dad."

"Does your father ever wash his hands?" the professor asked.

"He lives on a farm," Angela replied somewhat huffily. "Of course he does."

"Does he wash his hands sometimes even when they look clean?"

"We all wash our hands before dinner. What is your point, please?"

"He washes his hands in such cases because he accepts germ theory," said Dr. Dunbar. "He understands that hand washing reduces exposure to disease-carrying organisms. Yet he cannot see the germs, and he cannot know that any one hand-washing has saved him from a particular illness. In the same way, much of our understanding of evolution is inferred from a number of observations but not definitively confirmed in any one instance."

"That's a nice analogy," Angela responded. "But germs are not as — they're not as charged a subject as evolution."

"Very true," answered the professor. "You say you respect your father. Does he respect you?"

"Of course," Angela replied. "Is this another leading question of yours?"

"Yes it is," said Dr. Dunbar. "If he respects you, then he might be willing to hear you out. You can try telling him that evolution *is* a theory, one of the greatest of all scientific theories, a theory that provides the most consistent explanation for many known facts."

"Yes but…"

"And you could say that while the tremendous variety in tomatoes and cattle is in large part the result of human intervention over centuries — microevolution — nature has been at her job for millennia — macroevolution. Look at this orchid!"

Three petals of shimmering gold framed a red-tongued stamen. "*Lepanthes* — one of

my favorites," Dr. Dunbar said softly. "Orchids are the largest family of flowering plants in the world, found on every continent except Antarctica," she said with her eyes on the monitor. "Depending on who's doing the counting, there are 15,000–20,000 species — one of the most evolved groups of flowering plants. Look at this one. *Bletilla striata*. Chinese ground orchid. It grows in my mother's backyard in St. Louis."

Angela looked at the image as the professor continued. "Orchids vary in color, in fragrance, in structure. Each has a highly specialized relationship with the insects or birds that pollinate it. Yet we can trace them all back to common ancestral plants, just as you might trace your own family's genealogy. Macroevolution in all its glory." Dr. Dunbar looked up at Angela. "Do you think this might convince your father?"

"Oh, probably not," the student replied.

"Why is that?"

"Because he believes what he believes." Angela pointed to the screen. "I like that one."

"*Sarcochilus ceciliae*. It has a magnificent slipper. Could you two at least keep talking?"

"Another one of your questions," said Angela. "I would hope so. Maybe I'll buy him an orchid for Father's Day."

CHAPTER 5

The science behind evolution

In 1859, Charles Darwin wrote "The giraffe, by its lofty stature, much-elongated neck, fore-legs, head, and tongue has its whole frame beautifully adapted for browsing on the higher braches of trees." A 1996 study of giraffe behavior calls this conclusion into question.

What science is

In 1902, Rudyard Kipling (1865–1925) published his *Just So Stories,* a collection that included such classics as "How the Camel got his Hump" and "How the Leopard got his Spots." The field of science concerned with evolution is sometimes said to have its own share of "just so" stories. One of them is about the giraffe.

"The giraffe, by its lofty stature, much-elongated neck, fore-legs, head, and tongue has its whole frame beautifully adapted for browsing on the higher branches of trees," wrote Charles Darwin (1809–1882) in his 1859 work *The Origin of Species.*[19] Darwin speculated that the giraffe that could reach higher compared to other giraffes — "even an inch above the others" — would be at an advantage and would be more likely to survive during periods of scarcity. Darwin's idea, or **hypothesis**, fitted well with facts known at the time about browsing mammals and also with his overall **theory** of evolution. Recently, however, a new hypothesis has been proposed to make sense of new observations.

This new hypothesis is that the giraffe's long neck is most useful not for browsing but for combat. Male giraffes fighting for dominance have been observed attacking each other using their necks and armored and horned heads as clubs. In such exchanges, they have been known to shatter bones and even kill each other. Scientists have documented that the winners of these combats more often mate with the available females; therefore, more

© Scotch Macaskill

Recent research reveals that giraffes often feed on leaves at or below shoulder height especially during the dry season when feeding competition is most intense. Such observations suggest that the feeding advantages of long necks are minimal and point to alternative evolutionary explanations, such as the role of the neck in competition for females.

of their traits (including the traits that affect neck length) endure in the gene pool of succeeding generations.

Scientists since Darwin's time have made new observations that are being used to argue against the old hypothesis. Through fossil evidence, they know that the modern giraffe evolved from antelope-like ancestors that lacked an especially long neck. They know that the males have unusually armored skulls and their necks are quite a bit longer than the necks of females. These factors suggest that natural selection may have worked to extend neck length especially in the males and for reasons having to do with the neck itself rather than overall body height. These new facts diminish the credibility of Darwin's hypothesis about giraffes.

Scientists also have learned through careful observation that giraffes mostly eat leaves at shoulder height. In dry season, when competition can be most intense, they tend to find their food at levels even closer to the ground. In other words, giraffes with long necks do not seem to benefit significantly from their ability to browse higher up in trees.

Darwin based his original hypothesis on observed facts, but further observation by many scientists has yielded evidence that undercuts his original idea and may replace it with another one that better fits the facts as they are known today. Yet the old hypothesis has not been completely overthrown. Scientists note that the reason why a long neck has been maintained in giraffes may be different from the reason why it evolved in the first place. An advantage in reaching food may have played some early evolutionary role, but so might other factors as well. A long neck might have been an advantage for keeping an eye on predators, for example, or the extra surface area of a long neck may have offered an advantage in keeping cool.

The specific explanations may change as new observations are made, but the fact that giraffe necks have evolved is not in question. The explanation for why the giraffe has its long neck will continue to undergo refinement in the coming years, and this is an example of how **science** works.

Science is a *process* through which people seek a better understanding of the natural world around them. Science is about explaining physical phenomena through direct observations — through what can be seen, heard, tasted, smelled, and touched — and through inferences from those observations. Sometimes these observations are made through very advanced technology such as microscopy or telescopy, but they all boil down to direct observations.

Explanations that rely on claims not grounded in the physical world are outside of science. One could create a **fable** for why the giraffe got its long neck. For example, one could invent a story about how the first such creature wanted to see over an elephant's back. One could propose a supernatural explanation, such as that a divine creator chose to give the giraffe a long neck so that it could better reach up to heaven. These, however, would not be scientific explanations.

Although the process that we call "science" was not named until the 17th century, humans have been building a body of knowledge about the world around them for thousands of years of recorded history and surely for thousands of years before then. The hallmarks of today's scientific enterprise — curiosity, observation, and experimentation — are nothing new. Early humans were doing work that we would now call science when they learned how to find animals by following their tracks and leavings;

when they learned to anticipate the changing seasons by observing the sun, the moon, and the stars in the sky; when they figured out how to create fire; and when they learned how to fashion tools from bronze and iron.

Through observations of the natural world, our ancient ancestors understood many aspects of nature that became more refined modern sciences such as fluid dynamics, astronomy, and meteorology.

Our ancestors stumbled onto many discoveries about nature, and through trial and error, they observed that certain effects consistently occur from certain causes. They learned that water flows downhill, that the moon's appearance in the sky moves through phases, that falling air pressure feels a certain way and often precedes rain, and that cooked food is often easier to chew. The drive to understand propelled humans to seek out more discoveries and to combine discrete insights into explanations of how the world operates. Over time, certain methods have produced the most reliable insights, and these have been formalized into the process that we now call science.

Levels of scientific knowledge

Science begins with **data** collected through observation of the natural world. Data are observations and pieces of information. Observations that have been repeatedly confirmed are referred to as **facts**. Examples of scientific facts include the average distance between Earth and the sun (measured at 93 million miles), the number of protons in an atom of hydrogen and oxygen (one and eight, respectively), and the range of penguins (within the southern hemisphere and mostly within the polar region of that hemisphere). Though in casual conversation people use the word "fact" to mean something that is true and certain, in science, facts remain conditional, because there is always the possibility that contradictory evidence will be discovered. Data form the first tier of knowledge in science.

Hypotheses are tentative proposals to explain data — to explain why the observations are as they are. An hypothesis is tested by seeking other observations that either are consistent with the proposed explanation or that conflict with it. This testing can be done with controlled experiments or by further observations, either out in nature or in a laboratory. An hypothesis is falsified if careful observations conflict with its predictions. Though an hypothesis can be verified or discredited through testing, it can never be absolutely confirmed.

An example of an hypothesis is "all living organisms are made of cells." One prediction that flows from this hypothesis is that any living organism examined under the microscope will be seen as made up of cells. Over the centuries, scientists have examined countless organisms and found them all to have one or more cells. None have been found that are not cellular. Viruses are not made of cells; this observation would contradict the hypothesis if viruses were classified as living. Because viruses do not have their own metabolism and depend on the host cells they infect to reproduce, they are not considered living, and so the hypothesis remains credible.

A scientific **theory** is a comprehensive explanation of how nature works that encompasses many individual, tested hypotheses. A theory explains a diverse range of observations, offers predictions that can be tested, and has not been contradicted by valid evidence. According to the theory of general relativity, mass and energy curve space-time, resulting in the phenomenon known as gravity. According to the theory of quantum mechanics, subatomic particles behave like waves and particles simultaneously. According to the theory of evolution, the species that have populated Earth have changed over time and are all descended from a common ancestor.

Each of these theories has unanswered questions at their margins that scientists continue to explore (What is the ultimate source of gravity? Do black holes defy the tenets of quantum theory? What is the pace of evolution?). Yet all three theories are considered bedrock science by the scientific community because they each explain a diverse range of observations, offer predictions that can be tested, and have not been contradicted by valid evidence. At the same time, all scientific theories are tentative and can never be more than that. They are not "provable" in the absolute sense with which mathematicians or the public uses the word.

Skepticism is the prevailing attitude scientists take toward each other's work. Whenever a scientist presents new findings, he or she faces a gauntlet of critical examination from peers. Scientists repeat each other's experiments to see if they get the same results; they seek to disprove ideas by conducting new experiments that might yield contradictory evidence; they propose alternative hypotheses that might better explain a given range of facts. When hypotheses and theories stand up to such challenges, they gradually earn acceptance. If they are sufficiently novel, they transform the way that scientists think about a natural process. The scientific community, through its professional meetings and journals, passes judgment on the reliability of hypotheses and theories.

In the modern era, this theory-building process has been called the **scientific method**. While the particular observational and laboratory methodologies of the various sciences from astronomy to zoology differ in the details, they all follow the broad outlines just described. And, they all are employed in pursuit of the same goal: to explain the structures and processes of the natural world in the form of theories that make sense of all observations and predict the kinds of observations that will be made in the future.

Science is a dynamic process. Even a well-supported theory may lead to observations that are not easily explained by the theory. Such observations can stimulate the proposal of new hypotheses and new tests. This can result in a refinement of the original theory or in the abandonment of the original theory in favor of another theory.

Photo by Brian Prechtel, USDA, ARS, IS Photo Unit

Experimentation is one of the distinguishing steps in the scientific process.

When Gregor Mendel's (1822–1936) work in genetics came to the attention of other scientists, it was thought to be a rival to Darwinian evolution by natural selection as an explanation of biological diversity. Then biologists came to recognize that genetics provided an explanation for the origin of variety and continuity of features in reproduction. Darwin had observed these things but could not explain them. The introduction of genetics into Darwinian evolutionary theory transformed it into a more robust theory, what is sometimes called the **modern synthesis** in evolution.

The construction of knowledge about evolution

As stated earlier, data occupy the lowest tier of knowledge in science. In *The Origin of Species,* Darwin included the following data about domestic pigeons, based on his own detailed observations of the pigeons he raised, visits to pigeon breeders, and correspondence with these breeders:

> *In the skeletons of the different breeds, the development of the bones of the face differs enormously. The vertebrae vary in number; as does the number of the ribs, together with their relative breadth and the presence of processes. The number of the primary wing and caudal feathers, the relative length of the wing and tail, the relative length of the leg and foot, the development of skin between the toes, are all points of structure which are variable. The period at which the prefect plumage is acquired varies, as do the shape and size of the eggs, the manner of flight, and in some breeds the voice and disposition. Lastly, in certain breeds, the males and females have come to differ in a slight degree from each other.*[20]

Darwin's research on domestic pigeons showed that even very different breeds could be descended from a common ancestor.

Reflecting on his information about pigeons, Darwin wondered, from where did all these breeds come? Then he formulated his hypothesis: "Great as are the differences between the breeds of the pigeon, I am fully convinced that all are descended from the rock-pigeon [rock dove] *Columba livia.*"[21] Darwin then documented more facts in support of this hypothesis, including the fact that crossing pigeons from two distinct breeds created young that also could reproduce. This was evidence that even very different looking doves belonged to the same species. No facts collected in the century and a half that followed have contradicted Darwin's original hypothesis. Darwin combined tested hypotheses about pigeons with many other tested hypotheses to form his theory of evolution.

Within evolutionary theory today, there are many competing hypotheses about the details. For example, scientists have noted that there are very few ocean-dwelling insects. Of the estimated 2 million species of insects living today, less than 350 of them exist in or on the open ocean, in or near the spray of ocean water, or in tide pools. Why is this? Does it have to do with the salinity of ocean water, instability created by waves or tides, the pressure of water, or the dearth of oxygen at depth?

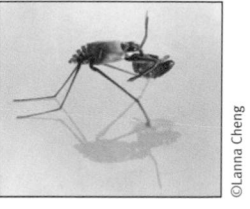
Of the 2 million described species of insects, only about 300 are regularly exposed to sea water and only five, such as the "Sea skater," exist on the open sea.

Such hypotheses have been proposed, and so has the hypothesis that insects have not become abundant in the ocean because there's no room for them there. Fossil records show that water-dwelling **crustaceans** existed for about 150 million years before any marine animals made the transition onto the uninhabited land (crustaceans include the modern species of shrimp, crab, lobster, and barnacles). Over the next 50 million years, descendents of those early land settlers diversified and became abundant. By the time insects emerged from those lineages, the marine niche had long been filled.

As was explained earlier, an hypothesis is stated in such a way that predictions can be made from it and tested, to see if they hold up, either through laboratory experiments or further observations in nature. For example, consider the hypothesis that some fundamental aspect of insects make them unable to withstand high pressure, which would explain why they are not found at ocean depth. To test this, scientists can observe insects in pressure boxes, and they can look for insects that can withstand high pressure. Indeed, one insect has been found that lives at 1,300 meters, at about 2,000 pounds per square inch of absolute pressure. This piece of evidence weighs against the pressure hypothesis.

Certainty and uncertainty

If there is one certainty in science, it is that nothing in science is certain. Although increasingly accurate accounts of nature have been achieved through science, definitive claims cannot be made. Scientists act on the assumption that there will always be new data to be discovered.

Scientists must remain flexible and open to new information, and they must always strive toward improved understanding. Indeed, along virtually

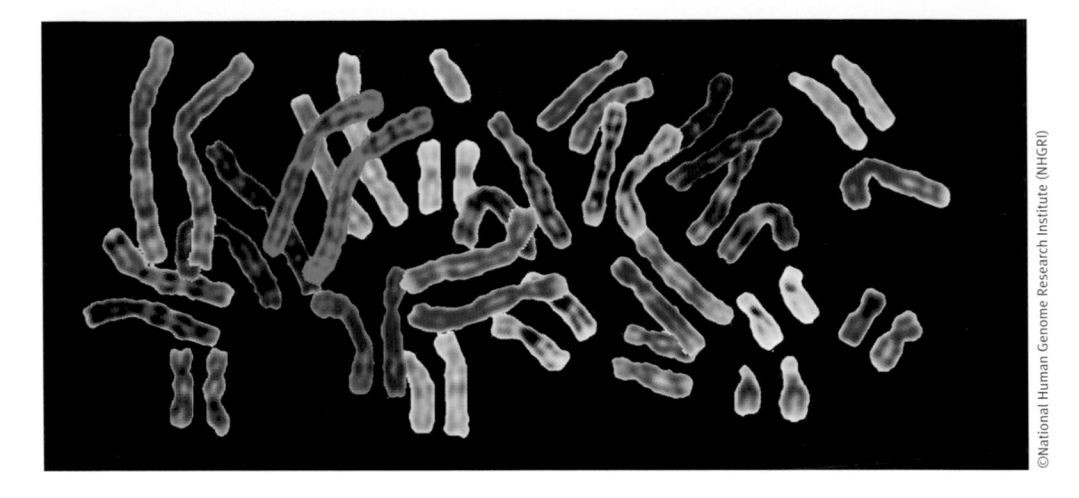

Although chromosomes were first discovered in the mid-1800s, it was not until the 1950s that an accurate count of human chromosomes was achieved.

every avenue of inquiry that scientists have pursued, scientific knowledge has evolved. Here are just two examples:

• Chromosomes (the structures inside cells that hold the genes) were first discovered in the mid-1800s. In the 1920s, staining techniques allowed scientists to count them. They counted 48 chromosomes in the human cell. By the 1950s, better observational technology helped scientists see more clearly inside the cell. They learned that the chromosomes had been mis-counted before and that the actual number was only 46.

• The theory of continental drift was first proposed in 1912 by geologists Alfred Wegener (1880–1930) and Frank Taylor (1860–1939). This is the proposition that 200 million years ago the Earth had one giant continent that broke and drifted apart. Several lines of evidence were employed to support the theory: the fit of the continents to each other like puzzle pieces; the similarity of fossils found in the bulging eastern coast of South America and the inward-curving western coast of Africa; the similarity in rock sequences along these two continents; data on ancient climates; evidence that the Earth's polar regions were once further toward the equators; and more. Yet this theory was not well received by other scientists because it did not provide an acceptable account of the mechanism by which continents moved. By the 1960s, scientists had made sufficient discoveries about the effects of convection currents on the sea floor and the magnetic properties of rocks to support a theory of plate tectonics. This new theory explained how movements of the crust of the Earth could account for drifting continents.

Indeed, throughout the history of science, there are numerous examples of theories that were initially resisted by the scientific establishment and that are accepted today as reliable depictions of nature. Quantum theory, which explains the behavior of matter and energy in the subatomic world, was once described as "weird science." Even Albert Einstein (1879–1955) doubted it. But it has prevailed because it best fits the experimental evidence amassed over the years by Max Planck (1858–1947), Niels Bohr (1885–1947), Einstein himself, and many other physicists. It became accepted because it coherently explained a range of observations that were inconsistent with previous theories and it could successfully predict additional data.

Within his own lifetime, Darwin saw the scientific community accept his theory of evolution. This happened because the theory coherently explained a range of observations and could successfully predict additional data. The evolutionary mechanism he proposed, natural selection, did not find acceptance until supportive evidence became available through the new field of genetics. Scientific acceptance of a theory usually builds slowly, in response to the creativity and hard work of many people who pool together their observations, experimental results, and analytical brainpower.

Non-scientific interpretations of science

Scientists seek to be rational and impartial. They work to prevent their own biases or personal motives from coloring their observations or analysis of data. Scientists are also full human beings with emotions as well as intellect. They do not leave behind their feelings just because they have put on a lab coat or started sifting through the dirt for fossils. All you have to do is see a scientist celebrating the completion of a successful experiment or reporting on a new theoretical insight to know that there is passion involved in science.

Plus, every person operates with a worldview — with a particular set of ideas about how things work and the meaning of existence. An individual's upbringing, personality, and surroundings help form his or her viewpoint. At best, this viewpoint is informed by what science has discovered about the universe and nature. However, such viewpoints can have a negative impact on the scientific enterprise in two ways.

A person's worldview can be so narrow, inflexible, and committed to some earlier understanding of the world that it obscures what science has discovered and impedes the person's ability to gain new insights about nature. A second way that worldview can have a negative impact on science is when a person claims scientific support for elements of his or her worldview that are not scientific; for example, when a person asserts that science supports his or her atheism or theism. The negative impact that

An individual's upbringing, personality, and surroundings help form his or her viewpoint.

such a position has is that, especially if the person holding it is a scientist; it gives the unwarranted impression that science answers philosophical or religious questions.

Yet it seems that humans will almost inevitably select particular scientific findings and interpret them to assert broader philosophical or religious views. The evidence for evolution has been interpreted many ways, in support of differing worldviews. Some interpretations emphasize the competitive and predatory nature of evolution, while others highlight its adaptive and cooperative features. Evolution has been viewed as a story of progress, with species engaged in an upward march through time. It also has been described as purposeless and directionless. It has been cast both as a glorious unfolding drama and as a messy and inefficient process. For some people, evolution is the story of how God works through natural laws to create the diversity of life and especially the human beings with whom God is said to have a unique relationship. For others, evolution bears witness that humans are intimately related to all other life forms. For still others, it is a testament to humanity's solitude in an indifferent universe. These are all non-scientific interpretations of evolutionary science.

Here are two examples of corresponding scientific and non-scientific interpretations:

Example 1. *Scientific:* The Earth appears to be 4.6 billion years old, which is long enough for humans to have evolved through natural processes from the first living organisms. *Non-scientific:* Humans are the aim and goal of the evolution of life on Earth. (Intention cannot be revealed through the scientific method.)

Example 2. *Scientific:* The DNA code is essentially the same for all living organisms on Earth due to their common descent from a single ancestor. *Non-scientific:* The fact that all living organisms share the DNA code is evidence of a divine creator who works from a single blueprint. (Science cannot address

Evolution Dialogues

whether a divine force was involved in evolution, because divine forces do not have to be predictable and do not have to obey natural laws.)

Non-scientific interpretations of science have their place, but it is not within science. Science is the quest for explanations of how things work based on natural processes and structures. The best science requires imagination, discipline, patience, perseverance, humility, and sometimes courage. But in the end, the scientist always returns to nature to test his or her ideas about nature.

Science is also a collective endeavor. Scientists operate within an established system for testing ideas. It is the expected practice of scientists to share their findings and conclusions with each other through peer-reviewed publications and presentations at scientific societies. They check each other's work, reconfirm or disconfirm observations, and critique each other's analyses. Ideas that are contradicted by data are rechecked; if contradictory data outweighs the supportive data, the idea may be reformulated or rejected outright. Ideas that have not been discredited remain in the pool. When everyone weighs in on the evidence, it increases the likelihood that the personal bias of any one individual will be balanced out.

What science is not

There is a term for a basic principle that undergirds scientific practice. It is **methodological naturalism**, and it is the assumption that explanations provided by science should make reference only to nature itself.

Methodological naturalism is often confused with a philosophical position, one that is outside the domain of science. This is called

Scientists seek natural explanations for natural events.

ontological naturalism. According to this philosophy, only the natural world exists. People who think this way are sometimes called **material reductionists** because they reduce all interpretations of the world to material processes (activities of matter and energy) and they deny the existence of any other possible sources of understanding.

So, for example, a materialist view of physics is that every action that occurs can be explained exclusively through atomic interactions. Taken another step, a materialist view of string theory — a relatively new branch of physics — is that everything that happens including atomic interactions is due solely to the vibrations of filaments inside fundamental particles such as protons and quarks. A materialist view of neuroscience is that consciousness is exclusively a by-product of the firing of networks of neurons in the brain. A materialist view of human behavior is that love is no more than an adaptive strategy that enhances survival and therefore has been preserved in the human genome through evolutionary processes.

Materialist viewpoints are often presented as science and are sometimes asserted by scientists, but their subjective and exclusivist nature puts them outside of science. Because these sorts of views are more closely related to questions about the meaning of nature, some people put them into a category they call "science as religion."

Science is *not* the only way of knowing. It is a way of knowing based on information attained through human interaction with the natural world. That is all. Science cannot by definition answer questions about the ultimate meaning of things, such as why are we here or what is the purpose of life. Wearing their scientific hats, scientists are obliged to stand mute before such questions, even though in other roles they may have much to say.

Evidence from science can be — even ought to be — employed in attempts to understand the meaning and purpose of things, but the ruminations themselves are not part of the scientific enterprise. How should society's goods be distributed? What should we do with this criminal? How should we raise our children? What can we do to be happier and more fulfilled? Such deliberations fit outside science. They belong to other ways of understanding the world, in such realms as philosophy, religion, and art.

FURTHER READING

The Advancement of Science: Science without legend, objectivity without illusions, Philip Kitcher (Oxford University Press, 1995)

Benchmarks for Science Literacy, AAAS (Oxford University Press, 1993)

Science for All Americans, F. James Rutherford and Andrew Ahlgren; AAAS (Oxford University Press, 1990)

The Structure of Scientific Theories, Frederick Suppe, ed. (University of Illinois Press, 1979)

What Science Is and How It Works, Gregory Derry (Princeton University Press, 2002)

Christian worldviews

Angela Rawlett was surprised to find she had finished her biology exam well before the class was over. She stood on the steps of the science building, staring at a landscape transformed by spring blooming. With 20 minutes to spare, she decided to go to her next class by a route that would take her through the campus gardens.

A small amphitheater was situated at the near side of the gardens. As Angela approached it, she saw a man sitting on one of the surrounding park benches, leaning on a briefcase set on his lap and sipping from a travel mug. She recognized Phil Compton, the campus minister who counseled her.

"Hey there," she said. "Do you always drink your morning coffee here?"

"Why hello, Angela," Phil said. "I'm sorry I can't offer you some."

"You should know by now that I don't drink coffee," the student answered. "But I have a water bottle." She pulled it out from her backpack.

Phil moved over on the bench to make room for Angela. "It's so nice out today that I left a note on the board for my senior seminar to meet here," he said.

"You teach?" Angela slung her backpack onto the ground and sat down next to the minister.

"Just one course a semester," he said. "In the religious studies department."

"You don't say," said Angela. "I didn't know that. What's the course about?"

"Doctrinal divisions. We're exploring the question of whether differences in Christian belief and practice are the devil's work, so to speak, or the inevitable outcome of discipleship. Are you on your way somewhere?"

"Eventually," Angela replied. "I just finished a bio test. I think I aced it, but there was one really weird question."

Phil looked at her with curiosity.

"In the extra credit section," Angela explained. "We had to select a trait and create a testable hypothesis for how it may have evolved through natural selection. I picked eyesight. But one of the choices was religiosity. Isn't that weird? To think of faith like it's a trait to be selected for?"

Phil smiled. "That reminds me of an article I read. It said dogs evolved soft eyes and the habits of licking our faces and hanging around at our feet because that's how they get food and shelter."

"I love my Fletcher so much, I would hate to think he doesn't love me back at least a little," responded Angela.

"And I my Aquinas," said Phil.

"Your dog?" asked the student.

"My cat," replied the minister.

The pair was silent a moment as they watched some students enter the garden and begin tossing around a Frisbee. "I can't believe that scientists have learned enough about genes to give them any credit for our religious leanings," said Angela.

"It's an area of research at least," answered Phil. "There may be a plausible explanation of religion as a product of cultural development. Cognitive processes and the genes that underlie that development would constitute just one part of the explanation." He paused and looked up at the cloudless blue sky. "But so what if we are able to explain how the love of God is mediated in the evolved brain? What does it say about the truth of that love?"

Angela looked up at the sky, too. "Like maybe God wired us to have faith."

"Maybe it happened like that," Phil said.

A Frisbee landed in a nearby bed of daffodils. Angela retrieved it and tossed it back to its owner. Returning to the bench, she said to Phil, "So tell me about doctrinal differences. Are they the devil's work?"

"You should know by now that I don't have answers," he said. "My job is to make students comfortable exploring the questions."

"That's evasive," said Angela, grinning. "You must have some opinion."

"I can confess it to you, since you're not in my seminar," answered Phil with a small smile. "I tend to believe that the different meanings and methods we put into baptism, for example, keeps us talking about baptism, which is what God wants us to do."

"You don't think there's one true way to baptize and all others are heretical?"

"No, on that issue I'm relatively easy. I take a harder line on other questions of doctrine. The reality of the trinity, for example."

"But that can't be proven."

"What need do I have of proof? The trinity is where my understanding of God begins, not where it ends."

"It would be nice, to answer the doubters," Angela argued. "If we had some ... some real records. It would be nice if we could just prove that Jesus existed as God on Earth. Or if we could prove God exists, for that matter."

"There are many philosophical proofs of God, but at the end of the day, none of them are adequate," responded Phil. "Human nature is such that God in the flesh could come knocking at the door and we wouldn't recognize her." He set down his travel mug and added, "By the way, what testable hypothesis did you come up with for the evolution of eyesight?"

"I said if eyes have evolved in response to environments where light exists, then we could expect that in environments where there is no light — such as in the darkest subterranean caves — we would expect to find creatures that have never evolved eyesight — or that have lost the ability to see."

"Not bad," said Phil. "I suppose one quick Google search would tell us if such creatures exist. What sort of testable hypothesis could you make for the evolution of religiosity?"

"I have no idea," said Angela. "That's why I didn't pick that trait. But let me think." She took a deep breath of the morning air. "Maybe ... maybe in environments where humans have perfect knowledge we would expect them not to have evolved faith because it would have provided no advantage."

"Interesting," said the minister. "Where could we look for such humans? In subterranean caves, perhaps?"

"Not on this campus at least," Angela quipped. She looked at her watch and stood up, heaving her backpack over her shoulder. "Ask your seniors that question, would you? Where are humans with perfect knowledge?"

CHAPTER 6

Christian worldviews

©Biblical Archaeology Society, Washington, D.C.

The "James Ossuary," first thought by its inscription, to be that of James, the brother of Jesus, was subsequently judged by the Israeli Antiquities Authority to be a forgery.

Defining Christianity

In 2002, an astounding historical discovery was announced. An Israeli antiquities collector was claimed to have in his possession an ossuary — a container for the bones of the dead — with an Aramaic inscription on the side, "Yaakov bar Yoseph, Achui de Yeshua." This translates as "James, son of Joseph, brother of Jesus."[22]

Two different authorities authenticated the box as dating from around the first century A.D. James, Joseph, and Jesus were relatively common names in that era, yet statistically the relationship described by the inscription would have been much less common. Based on this evidence, the ossuary was declared to be the first archaeological discovery ever to corroborate biblical references to Jesus.

Yet within a short time, the ossuary turned from an article of veneration into an object of ridicule. In 2004, five alleged conspirators were indicted by Israel for running a forgery ring. They were accused of doctoring authentic historical artifacts to make them appear more valuable than they truly were. The James ossuary was exposed as a fake.

This scandal sent shockwaves through the Near Eastern archaeological community, threatened the livelihood of antiquities dealers, and damaged the reputations of scholars who had vetted the fraudulent artifacts. Yet the saga of the James ossuary has had little or no effect on most Christians. This is because the faith they put in the reality of Jesus is not primarily dependent on material evidence.

114

Foundations of Christianity

The starting points for Christian belief are in a set of writings. These texts were written by a variety of authors over a long time period and then formally assembled in the first centuries of the Christian community into one collection called the **Bible**. The Bible includes works from the sacred texts of Judaism, which Christians refer to as the Old Testament. It also includes a set of books that contain accounts of Jesus' life (the Gospels), a history of the early Christian communities, discussions about the nature of God and other religious questions (theology), and personal correspondence. Christians call this second section of the Bible the New Testament.

The Bible is filled with stories. There are the Old Testament stories: the creation of the world, the origin of the first man and woman and their expulsion from paradise, and the triumphs and tribulations of a people who came to be called the Jews, who are presented as those through whom God chose to reveal the nature of the divine and divine purpose. There also are the New Testament stories: of events in Jesus' life, the parables he told, and the religious vision he taught. The Christian religion begins with faith or trust that these stories reveal universal paradigms for human meaning and living.

A **revelation** is a basic insight that orients a person's understanding. It may result from the acquisition of a new piece of information, like the key piece in a puzzle, or it may occur like a sudden shift in perspective, where information already known is seen in a new way. Revelation is a term most common to the western monotheistic religions but is functionally comparable to **enlightenment** in eastern religious traditions. The term is also used in a secular sense when a scientist says that the study of nature reveals some basic feature of nature; for example, the ecological interdependency of species.

Revelation is an essential dimension of Christian knowledge, but it is not the only one. It is commonly said that Christians also recognize truth through their **traditions**, their **reason**, and their **experience**. These four sources of Christian knowledge are not isolated from one another but are mutually dependent, and each rests on particular assumptions or faith commitments.

Tradition is the accumulation of biblical interpretations, theological concepts, forms of church government, and religious practices that are passed down within the Christian community through the generations. In the Roman

Catholic Church, for example, tradition has created a hierarchy of teaching authorities, with the pope as the head of the church. In other branches of Christianity, the highest teaching authority is the local congregation as a group. Tradition accounts for the persistence of particular expressions of Christianity such as the Nicene Creed, which has been the most widely used declaration of Christian belief since the fourth century. Tradition determines who may serve as a religious leader and whether and what kind of adornments may be placed in churches or used in worship. Tradition is what has determined which ancient writings should be included in the Bible. Regardless of the particular history of any tradition, Christians believe that it has been directed in some manner by God.

Tradition is a source of Christian knowledge that influences, among many other things, what adornments are placed in churches, forms of worship, and who may lead the community.

The role of reason as a foundation for Christian knowledge has been debated by Christians as long as the community has existed. Some early theologians argued that Christians do not need to buttress their faith with reason because God has already revealed all that is necessary through the Bible. Others respond that reason is a gift from God that lends understanding to faith. According to this latter perspective, reason must be applied to interpret the Bible and the tradition in light of life's ongoing circumstances. Of course, tradition itself, including the determination of what constitutes the Bible, is in part a product of reason.

Christianity has had many great thinkers throughout its history — Athanasius (296–383), Augustine (354–430), Thomas Aquinas (1225–1274), and Martin Luther (1483–1546), to name only four — who through their carefully reasoned theological writings have had a profound influence on how the Bible is understood and Christianity practiced. But the exercise of reason in Christianity is about more than individual scholarship. All sorts of organized gatherings — synods of the Evangelical Lutheran Church, councils of Orthodox bishops, annual meetings of the Southern Baptist Convention, and the like — involve people reasoning together to interpret and understand the meaning of the Bible in the context of a particular historical tradition.

Experience, another foundational component to Christian knowledge, occurs within at least three contexts. There is what is called religious experience or experience of God. This can be an emotionally powerful sense of the presence of God. It can be an "ah ha!" experience of religious insight or revelation. Or, it can be a profound sense of comfort in the midst of life's trials. Although such experiences can happen at any time, they often occur in conjunction with activities such as prayer, meditation, pilgrimage, song and chant, and retreat.

A second context of experience is mundane living in the everyday world. The Bible includes many images drawn from ordinary daily experience; for example, father, neighbor, and sower. These images serve as powerful metaphors through which often-complex religious ideas are expressed.

The third context of experience is what comes from the application of reason to our observations of the world — what today is the world experienced through science. One of the most momentous events in the history of humanity was when Galileo turned his telescope to the night sky. He observed what no human being had ever seen before: mountains and valleys on the moon, satellites revolving around Jupiter, and phases of the evening star, Venus. These observations helped convince him that Copernicus was correct when he proposed that the Earth moved around the sun, in contradiction to the long-held belief that the Earth was the center of God's universe.

Galileo's discovery revealed that not only the venerable 1,000-year-old science of his day, but also understanding of the meaning of the Bible, could be mistaken in a literal sense (without calling into question the text's theological meaning). Reason sometimes overturns religious assumptions in this way, but sometimes it adds new evidence to underscore traditional beliefs. For example, modern cosmologists have learned that the universe is a great deal bigger than previously estimated. For Christians who use science to inform their faith, this finding amplifies the sense of God's cosmic embrace as described in Psalm 147, in which the God "counts the number of the stars and calls them all by their names."

©Ron Wayman, Tampa, FL; NASA

Galileo was the first person to observe mountains and valleys on the moon.

He also was the first to see five of Jupiter's moons, including Callisto (below). These observations encouraged him to adopt Copernicus' sun-centered model of the universe.

Credit: NASA

The Christian story

The apparent indifference of most Christians to the controversy over the James ossuary, exhibiting a freedom from the need for empirical confirmation of Jesus' existence, is ironic because **Christianity** understands itself to be a historical **religion**, that is, one that stems from an interpretation of events said to have actually occurred 2,000 years ago. The story is well known to Christians from the four tellings included in the Christian Bible and attributed to the authors of the first four New Testament books, the Gospels: Matthew, Mark, Luke, and John. Jesus is described as being born in humble circumstances to a Jewish family from Nazareth, of peasant origins yet with noble roots, and trained as a carpenter. As a young man he was baptized, entered a brief period of fasting and reflection, and then emerged as an itinerant rabbi and healer.

According to this story, Jesus preached a vision of God's love for every person and of God's call for people to love God and one another. At the same time, Jesus criticized laws and religious rituals that he believed interfered with the expression of such love. For this reason, he was viewed as a threat to the social order and so he was arrested, tried, and condemned to death. He was crucified, as was the common practice for execution of rebels and other criminals in those days, and then buried in a tomb contributed by a wealthy patron. The Gospels relate that, three days later, Jesus appeared in the flesh to his disciples and that after 40 days he was taken up to be with God. Christians hold that faith in Jesus, as the one who reveals who God is, is the foundation of human hope for the meaningfulness of existence.

Christian belief and history

The preceding is the story that is carried forth in the Christian faith. What is documented historically is that disciples of Jesus declared him to be the **Messiah** or **Christ** (these words translate as "the anointed one" and imply that Jesus is God's chosen one). The disciples were inspired to preach Jesus' **gospel** ("good news") of God's love. Through the efforts of the disciples and other early converts, Christianity spread among Jews and especially

118

among non-Jews in the Greco-Roman world. Today it is the world's largest and most widespread religion, with an estimated 2 billion adherents from all parts of the globe.

Although there are various theological points on which Christians will disagree, a general summary of their central convictions is as follows: Christians believe that their call is to love God and live with compassion for others, following the example of Jesus of Nazareth, whom they revere as their "Lord and Savior." They believe that by following the example of Jesus, they are enabled to live in communion with God and their fellow human beings. They believe that nothing, including death, can separate them from eternal communion with God through Jesus.

Christians recognize that they often do not act in love following Jesus' example — that they sin. They believe that they are nonetheless loved by God. Therefore, they hold that, if they conscientiously confess their wrongdoing, God will forgive them and accept them as restored to loving communion. They also hold that a commitment to redress the harm they have caused through their sin and an active effort to avoid evil behavior in the future are expressions of genuine confession.

Jesus' death by crucifixion is understood as the sign of the ultimate human rebellion against God. Jesus' resurrection is understood as the confirming sign that reconciliation with God is possible even in the face of such rebellion. The example of Jesus' life and service to the needs of others is taken as the model for all persons to follow, showing them how to relate to God and participate fittingly in the world that God is creating.

As the first Christian believers organized themselves into religious communities, questions arose as to the relationship between Jesus and God. This provoked such dissension that, by the fourth century, the Roman emperor Constantine called together a meeting of Christian leaders (bishops) to decide the question. Their conclusion, based on biblical and other writings, was that God is a **trinity**, or three-in-one: Father, Son, and Holy Spirit. However, there is a small portion of the Christian community that does not subscribe to the consensus view of a Trinitarian God.

The fourth century Roman Emperor Constantine called together the first universal council of the Christian community at Nicaea in 325.

There also has been debate since the early centuries of the Christian community about the divine and human natures of Jesus. A fifth century council of the whole Christian church affirmed that Jesus, while having a divine nature, also had a fully human nature.

There are many ways that Christians diverge in belief and practice. Some Christians object to strictly masculine referents for the Trinity and have suggested alternatives such as "Creator, Redeemer, and Sanctifier" (this particular phrase has in turn triggered debate about whether the persons of the trinity can be identified with distinctive roles). Some Christians baptize infants and others only adults. Some Christian churches allow men and women to serve as clergy, while others only allow men and, in some of those places, the men must be unmarried.

Christians have organized themselves into major groupings such as Eastern Orthodox, Roman Catholic, and Protestant. Further subdivisions of these major groups, known as **denominations**, number in the many hundreds: Anglican, Baptist, Presbyterian, Methodist, Byzantine Catholic, and the like. In addition, there are many local Christian communities that operate outside a formal denominational structure. Each denomination or group may have its own set of teachings about beliefs (**doctrines**), its own formal statements of religious belief (**creeds**), and its own distinctive worship practices (**liturgies**). They also may vary in the number and form of their ceremonial practices (**rites**). However, the object of all Christian activity is to understand God's will and be faithful to it.

Indeed there is such incredible diversity within the Christian tradition that it has been said the only way to determine whether persons are Christian is to ask them and see what they say. Of course, this self-identifying method does not really work for a number of reasons, not least of which is the fact that some Christians refuse to recognize as true Christians other self-proclaimed Christians whose tenets differ from their own.

Evolution Dialogues

Contexts of knowing

Christians believe that who Jesus is and that God is Creator are revealed to them through their sacred texts. But Christians do not always agree about specific interpretations of these beliefs. Tradition, reason, and experience all have an impact on these interpretations. Different emphases lead to different interpretations. Does such diversity mean that the expression, "Christian knowledge," is nonsense? Not necessarily. But it does suggest that all claims to Christian knowledge need to be expressed with considerable humility.

All the manifestations of Christianity have one thing in common with each other and also with all the other religions of the world. This is their concern for what lies at the foundation of the world and for humanity's relation to that "unseen order," to use a phrase from William James's (1842–1910) classic text, *The Varieties of Religious Experience.* The focus of religion, its context of knowing, is on what things *mean* rather than on what they *are*.

Different contexts of knowing require different forms of knowledge. A commonly used example is water boiling on a stove. A scientific explanation involving thermodynamics, the gas laws, and the chemistry of water can provide one explanation for the phenomenon. From the perspective of another context, boiling water on the stove can be explained by describing the action of a man filling a tea kettle and placing it on a lit stove burner. From another perspective, the phenomenon can be explained by describing the man's wife's desire for tea and their interpersonal relationship. None of the explanations supersedes the other. Each is appropriate to its context.

The consumption of bread and wine can be understood in terms of the biochemistry of nutrition, in terms of the sensual pleasure of eating, in terms of the conviviality of a meal shared with friends, or, as in the Christian context, as the reenactment of a particular supper that bears profound religious significance. Again, each context provides its own distinctive framework of explanation. And in no case does the explanation in one context necessarily invalidate the explanation in another.

Different contexts of knowing provide different, non-contradictory explanations for water boiling on a stove.

Defining religion

Religion is the pursuit of ultimate questions such as the purpose of life, proper ways to conduct one's life, the meaning of pain and suffering, the status of the person after death, and the nature of the divine. Religion, as far as we know, is a uniquely human project. It also is both an individual and a group endeavor, with religious insights shared and assessed within communities of faith and transmitted across cultural boundaries and over great spans of time.

Through religion, humans seek to understand depths of reality beyond the reach of scientific exploration. Explaining how it is distinct from **empirical inquiry**, Roman Catholic professor of theology John Haught writes, "In religious experience we do not so much grasp this depth as allow the depth to grasp us." According to Haught, "Religion exists only because beneath the surface of mundane experience, many people have felt — some more palpably than others — that something inexhaustibly important and mysterious is going on. At times the dimension of depth powerfully carries them away, and in doing so provides an unexpectedly solid grounding to their lives."[23]

Every known society in the history of the world has manifested religious behavior in some form, which suggests its essential connection with human nature. A scientific explanation of religion is that it is an adaptive cultural form that enhances survival on the group level. According to this hypothesis, shared belief in a divine power can reinforce commitment within the group. So, people may behave in ways that are individually disadvantageous — they behave altruistically — in order to reap the blessings and avoid the penalties that they believe will emanate from the divine

A scientific explanation for religion is that shared belief in and commitment to a higher power strengthens bonds within a group, which in turn improves the survival and reproductive potential of individual group members.

Evolution Dialogues

being. This altruistic behavior enhances the ability of a community to work together for survival.

Some people find a biological explanation of religion insufficient. For them, the apparently universal impulse toward religion, however it can be explained biologically, suggests the reality of the depth toward which it reaches. "Built into the human makeup is a longing for a 'more' that the world of everyday cannot requite," writes Huston Smith (1919–), a scholar on world religions. "This outreach strongly suggests the existence of the something that life reaches for in the way that the wings of birds point to the reality of air."[24]

Faith as the starting point

At first glance, it might seem that the difference between religion and science turns on the matter of faith. Christians believe in certain things for which there is no logical proof or material evidence. Yet, as the saying goes, you have to believe something in order to know anything. All knowledge systems depend on faith of some sort.

In mathematics, **axioms** (self-evident truths or common sense assumptions drawn from real-world experience) are the articles held on faith. Solutions to mathematical problems are built on such givens.

A classic example of a mathematical axiom was first devised by Euclid in ancient Greece. He asserted that in geometry, "the whole is greater than the part." Another basic assumption that underlies Euclidean geometry is: if A = C and B = C, then A = B. Given a set of axioms and definitions, Euclid was able to prove a number of mathematical statements, such as that the sum of the internal angles of a triangle is equal to two right angles or 180 degrees.

Mathematical assumptions determine particular systems of mathematical research.

Assumptions that are accepted in one system of mathematics may not be adopted in another. This changes what can be proved. For example, the proof that the interior angles of a triangle add up to 180 degrees works in plane geometry but is not true when the triangle is drawn on the surface of a sphere.

Biology rests on assumptions, such as that mathematics provides a true representation of relationships in nature and that a natural explanation can be provided for any natural event. Physics, chemistry, geology, astronomy, and all the other branches of science also share these and other assumptions.

Any system of knowledge is built communally — through shared assumptions, experiences, observations, and judgments of many people over time. For example, most educated people today accept the basic principles of genetic science without having ever seen any DNA. What any one individual knows about just about anything, therefore, is built upon a trust or faith in the accuracy of others' reports.

One of the major differences between science and religion is with respect to the expectation of change. There are certain assumptions that are necessary to do any science at all, for example, that the universe can be understood or that mathematics is a fruitful language with which to describe the universe. But confidence in the theories formed by science is conditional and so, in principle, always tentative and open to change. Generally, Christian religious communities tend not to expect that their theological theories or doctrines will change, although historically the particulars of doctrines have been challenged and doctrines have been reformed in response to such challenges. Another difference between science and religion is related to this view of change. Scientific theories both are frameworks in which to organize scientific inquiry and are themselves ideas to be deliberately tested. In one sense, the whole of the scientific enterprise is the testing of scientific theories. Although historically religious doctrines are tested due to cultural circumstances, there is not a deliberate tradition of theoretical or doctrinal testing. For many, it is this attitude toward testing that is the most significant difference between science and religion. This difference may be the one that lies at the heart of many of those historical moments that are viewed as conflicts between science and religion.

Translations of the Bible from several manuscripts and different original languages has resulted in some substantially different readings of the text.

Contested knowledge

In the past 2,000 years, there have been many different translations of the books comprising the Bible from the original Hebrew, Aramaic, and Greek. Certain passages have been included in some versions of the Bible but not in others, and some ancient whole books of a biblical nature were not included in the Bible at all. Christianity has been practiced by people of different cultures and eras following the traditions of their times and places. The dynamic relationship of revelation, tradition, reason, and experience explains why there is so much diversity within Christianity.

Galileo's convictions about the motions of the Earth spurred a controversy that has had a significant impact on the way that people understand how science and religion relate to one another. However, the Galileo controversy was not a simple contest between science and religion, as many eventually concluded. Rather, it was about the relative importance of the various sources of Christian knowledge. The church authorities of Galileo's time placed great weight on the authority of tradition for the interpretation of the Bible. Galileo held that reasoned observation of God's creation could help form a better interpretation of what is revealed and known through Christian tradition.

Another more contemporary example of the interplay between Christian sources of knowledge revolves around evolutionary theory. In some contexts, the controversy over evolution is between revelation and reasoned experience: between those who hold that each word of the Bible was inspired by God and so is literally true and those who hold that no part of the Bible is exempt from rational analysis in the light of contemporary experience of the world. In other contexts, it is a controversy between two understandings of tradition: one where tradition is viewed as a collection of fixed truths and another where tradition is viewed as a living, growing understanding of revelation that is constantly being transformed in the light of experience. In yet other contexts, it is a controversy between tradition and experience: a tradition that depicts God as Creator intervening in nature's history versus the experience of successful explanations of nature's history without reference to God.

Those who believe in biblical inerrancy hold that the Hebrew word in Genesis 1 that is translated as "day" must refer to a 24-hour period.

Central to these controversies is the question of what it means to be "literal." Some Christians hold to **biblical inerrancy** — the belief that the Bible contains no error of any sort and, to avoid introducing error, one must read the Bible using the contemporary, plain meaning of each word. For such readers of the Bible, the word "day" can only mean a 24-hour span of time and therefore God created humans in a single day — the sixth day of creation as told in Genesis. In the same way, the phrase in Genesis that God "breathed into his nostrils the breath of life" is taken to mean that the first human originated exactly as physically depicted in that line.

Other Christians believe in **biblical infallibility** — the belief that the Bible makes no mistakes in regard to what it teaches. For such readers, a literal meaning of the Bible can include metaphor, allegory, and parable. A "day" can be read to mean a cycle of time, and "breathed in … the breath of life" can be read to include the entire process of descent through evolutionary processes. Through this latter approach, Christians have been able to reconcile not only seeming conflicts between science and the Bible but also between the diverse biblical references to divine creation found in Genesis, Psalms, and Job.

In whatever manner religious knowledge relates to or interacts with scientific knowledge, it is a fact that many and perhaps most people around the globe rely on their religious understanding to sustain them through life. The equanimity with which the early Christians faced their deaths under persecution by Rome is one of the reasons that their religion grew so quickly. People wanted to have the knowledge those martyrs had.

Furthermore, the drive within Christianity to understand God and the world as created by God has been a major stimulus behind the acquisition of other types of knowledge over the past 2,000 years. Although Christianity has — like most other large-scale human enterprises — provoked human conflict, warfare, and other acts of evil, it also has inspired compassionate care of the sick and impoverished, development of moral codes and systems of justice, expansion of education, engagement in the arts, and the emergence of modern science.

FURTHER READING

Introduction to the History of Christianity, Tim Dowley, ed. (Augsburg Fortress Publishers, 2002)

The Oxford Illustrated History of Christianity, John McManners, ed. (Oxford University Press, 2001)

The world as explained by evolution

"Angela! Come down here! I want you to see this!"

College student Angela Rawlett saw the head of her advisor poking out from a doorway at the far end of a hallway in the science building. When she entered the room, she saw a large space filled with bookshelves, computer equipment, and several lab tables. Dr. Laurel Dunbar was bent over a large terrarium. Inside it was a jungle-like mixture of plants surrounded by moss, set against a backdrop of driftwood.

©Julie Mavity-Hudson, The Gesneriad Society

"What do you think?" asked the professor, obviously giddy with excitement. "I can't get to the greenhouse as often as I'd like, so I set this up. It keeps my spade in the dirt, so to speak."

Angela set her backpack on the floor, pulled up a lab stool, and peered through the glass to the horticultural landscape inside. "This is pretty cool," she said.

"Of course, I've got some orchids in here," said the professor. "*Masdevallia*, *dracula*, and *dendrobium* — plus some companions from their natural habitat — *tillandsias* and *cryptanthus*. None are flowering right now, but they should, Lord willing and I've got the conditions right."

Dr. Dunbar gave her terrarium a pat and turned toward the student. "I know we have to talk about your fall schedule today, but I just had to show this to you."

"I'm glad you did," responded her student. "It's got me psyched for plant biology."

"Psyched is good. You should register for that course," said Dr. Dunbar. "But you see now how it made sense to take Bio 122 first. You needed that introduction to evolution. Because as you know, one of the first topics we introduce in 224 is the evolution of plants."

"You're kidding," said Angela. "I thought I was going to be done with all that."

"Heavens no," said the professor, as she flashed a broad grin. "You're never done with evolution. It puts the rest of biology into perspective and explains many otherwise strange things. For example, endosymbiosis. You'll hit that early in the semester."

"Huh? Endosymbiosis?"

"The theory that explains the origin of chloroplasts in early eukaryotes by the engulfing of bacteria that were added and maintained in whole as parts of the cell, rather than digested."

Angela gave her a blank look. The professor explained, "The development of plants from more simple biotic life."

"Oh. The fact is, I'm a little annoyed at evolution right now."

"Really?" said Dr. Dunbar. "A spat! Tell me about it."

"This morning, Dr. Brown gave us a PowerPoint show about human origins," said Angela. "First he flipped pretty fast through early evolution: bacteria, multi-celled organisms, the first mammals, ancestors to the great apes, and pre-human ancestors. And then he showed us the branches of human species — *Australopithecus*, *Homo erectus*, and all the others, until finally he got to *Homo sapiens*."

"A pictorial history. What a lovely way to teach."

"It was neat," Angela admitted. "But it was also disturbing. I mean, it doesn't make humans seem very special."

"I don't know about that," said Dr. Dunbar. "I think we are pretty special."

Multi-celled organisms: fungi, plants, and animals.

"But you'd say the same thing about orchids," Angela protested. "What I mean is, where do humans start being humans? And what about those human species that died out? I didn't know about them before. What about them?"

"What about them?"

"Did they have souls? Were they made in the image of God?"

"Those are really interesting

Evolution Dialogues

questions," answered the professor. "Here's another: Why would God need to make all those practice species?" She looked hard at Angela and then added, "I don't mean to sound evasive, but these questions are not the kind that I, acting as a biologist, could ever address. Neither the soul nor God's image can be analyzed or understood using the scientific method. So as your science advisor, I am not comfortable speculating on such things vis-á-vis humans and other hominoids." An object on the shelf behind Angela caught the professor's attention. "Let me show you some really special creatures," she said.

Dr. Dunbar lifted from the shelf a wooden box covered by a lid of clear plastic. Inside it were about a dozen cardboard boxes, each holding an insect that was labeled and mounted on a pin.

Angela gazed down through the lid at a collection of bees, wasps, flies, and moths. "Do you know what these have in common?" the professor asked.

"They're all dead bugs?"

Dr. Dunbar smiled indulgently. "Each is known to pollinate a particular orchid. If my collection were truly representative, it would include bats and birds, too."

"What is that insect there, with the long curled tube off its face?" asked Angela.

"A most interesting specimen," said Dr. Dunbar. "That is a meganosed fly."

"Why in the world does it have such a long schnozz?"

"Such a long *proboscis*," answered the professor.

"So why does it have such a long ... such a long proboscis?"

"Co-evolution," answered the plant biologist. "Two species adapting to each other in such ways that leave them essentially reliant on the other. There are survival advantages to a plant that places its nectar deeply inside its floral tube and to a fly that can reach deeply for that nectar."

"But there must be disadvantages, too," said Angela. "I can't imagine such a little fly trying to cart that thing around."

"Excellent inference. There are indeed costs for the fly and costs for the flower. This too you will learn about in 122. Evolution, we are discovering, leads to some very complicated arrangements."

Dr. Dunbar replaced the box on the shelf. "Let's head down to my office. We need to look at the course catalog, because I'm thinking you ought to fit in a religion course next semester. That's where you could chew on your questions about the soul and the significance of human existence."

"I need to do something like that," responded Angela as they

Two organisms that evolve in relation to one another, like flowers and honey bees, are said to co-evolve.

walked together down the hall. "Sometimes I want to use other parts of my brain. I don't want to just learn about things; I want to learn what it all means." Angela stopped and looked urgently at her mentor. "And I have so many questions. Like, now you have me wondering about how humans relate to other living things."

"What do you mean?" Dr. Dunbar asked.

"Have we co-evolved in some way with the rest of creation, or do we stand apart?"

"In either case, does that make us special?"

"I don't know, but I wonder," said Angela. "One thing that might make us special is that we can *see* what's amazing about all of God's creatures. Like your orchids and bugs, you know? We can see the connections between all living things and how they are related. Maybe this ability to see is how we reflect the image of God. I wonder about these things."

CHAPTER 7

The world as explained by evolution

Diversity beyond measure

In 2003, a sailing yacht called the Sorcerer II set off on a three-year, round-the-world mission. Aboard were J. Craig Venter, a leading figure in the field of genetic sequencing, and several of his colleagues. They followed in the wake of Charles Darwin (1809–1882), who from 1831 to 1836 circumnavigated the globe as a naturalist on the H.M.S. Beagle.

Among the many things Darwin did on his journey was to collect a wide variety of plant and animal specimens that were previously unknown in the Western world. Darwin's finds, along with those collected by his contemporaries, helped scientists of the 19th century categorize species and get a better understanding of their relationships to each other. The journey was instrumental to Darwin and prompted him to conceive of his theory of evolution, which he first started to articulate a few years after he returned home from the voyage.

The goal of Venter's team on the Sorcerer II was to collect species like Darwin did, but instead of plants and animals, its focus was on **microbes**: on **viruses**, **bacteria**, and **archaea** (this last group includes single-celled organisms genetically distinct from bacteria that tend to live in extreme environments such as superhot or supercold water). Since microbes are invisible to the human eye and hardly even distinguishable under a microscope, the Sorcerer crew did not even try to collect intact samples. Rather, by taking up a few gallons of seawater every 200 miles and using a rather complicated filtering process, they collected just the **DNA** (deoxyribonucleic acid) from the organisms. They used a similar process to collect microbial DNA from soils, swamps, sulfur vents off the seafloor, and other promising locations.

Venter's goal for the voyage was to rack up DNA from as many as 100,000 new species and tens of millions of new genes. Indeed, on a trial

Visualization of a microbial protein intertwined with a DNA strand.

run in the Sargasso Sea near Bermuda — thought to be a virtual dead zone — he claims to have discovered at least 1,800 new species and more than 1.2 million new genes.

What is exciting about this adventure is that it could add so much to the relatively little that is currently known about microbes. Before Venter's journey, only about 6,000 microbial species had been identified even though organisms of this type are overwhelmingly present in the world. Their biomass (a measurement of living matter that correlates to weight) is thought to be at least equal to and probably greater than the biomass of all plants and animals.

Venter could not predict what new intellectual discoveries would result from his so-called "microbial global sampling expedition," but at the very least, it is helping scientists obtain a greater understanding of the diversity of species on Earth. "We will be able to extrapolate about all life from this survey," Venter declared in a magazine interview. "This will put everything Darwin missed into context."[25]

Venter may have overstated his claim, and certainly Darwin can be excused for having missed a few things when he first put forth his theory of evolution in 1859. Relatively few fossils had been recovered in the 19th century, nothing of DNA had been discovered, and naturalists had only begun to tally the vast number of the world's creatures. Since Darwin's time, too, there have been great advances in other relevant fields of science such as geology, biology, and even cosmology. As scientists have acquired new information, they have used it to refine their ideas about how evolution actually occurs. Even so, the more scientists learn, the more aware they are of the gaps in their knowledge base.

Venter himself acknowledged that despite his ambitious agenda and the sophisticated 21st century technology at his disposal, the Sorcerer II only captured a fraction of the world's microbial species. Indeed, the incredible richness of Earth's life may perhaps defy cataloging. Scientists to date have discovered and formally described around 1.8 million species — mostly mammals, birds, and plants — but most think the total out there is between 4 million and 15 million. Some even put the estimate at 100 million or more, considering all the microbes, **fungi, insects, protists**, and

Evolution Dialogues

other invisible and near-invisible forms of life. Even the large **mammals** have not been fully counted: a new species of mangabey monkey, *Lophocebus kipunjji*, was discovered in Tanzania as recently as 2005.

One big family

All of the species that have been identified thus far have one important characteristic in common: they all contain DNA, the "building blocks of life."[26] The reason that all living things have DNA is because it plays an essential biological role. Sections of DNA, operating in units known as **genes** and responding to environmental stimuli, carry instructions that tell cells to make proteins. Proteins in turn form the structure of new cells. They also form enzymes, which conduct essential activities such as building cell walls or converting nutrients to energy. Interacting with the environment, genes help mold each organism into its shape and behavior. Genes also serve as templates or a "library of recipes" that preserve the instructions that guide the development of an organism. They are the form of the inheritance that is passed down from one generation to the next.

Different species have different amounts of DNA, ranging from hundreds of thousands to billions of base pairs. Bacteria have relatively little DNA, for example. Yet more DNA does not necessarily mean more complex: salamanders have more DNA than humans, and so do rice and wheat. What makes each organism unique is not quantity of DNA but what DNA it has and how and when that DNA is activated in its environment.

In recent decades, scientists have learned how to decode the DNA inside cells of organisms, and this has revealed an astounding fact: the order of the molecules called "base pairs" strung along the DNA (the **DNA sequence**) is remarkably similar between species. For example, the base pair sequence of human DNA is about 99 percent identical to that of a chimpanzee and about 85 percent identical to that of a mouse. The differences that can be seen in the physical and behavioral appearances of humans, chimpanzees, and mice are due to the relatively few genes that are different as well as to different ways that the shared genes express themselves.

According to the theory of evolution, all species stem from a common ancestor, and this is what explains the likenesses in the DNA of distinct species. That ancient, original ancestor passed its DNA to its descendants, and they to their descendants. In each generation, small changes in the DNA were introduced through the processes of **mutation** and **recombination**. Most of these changes are neutral and unaffected by natural selection for the most part. A much smaller number of mutations are adaptive or mal-

Human DNA is more similar to chimpanzee DNA than to that of mice, indicating that humans share a more recent common ancestor with chimpanzees.

adaptive. The neutral and adaptive changes accumulate down through the generations. Over millions of years and across changing environments, this has created the similar yet distinct lines of DNA found in different species today.

Darwin did not know about DNA, genes, mutations, or recombination, but he did understand variation. Since his time, scientists have begun to understand how changes at the DNA level can generate a tremendous array of biological variation. As just noted, most introduced changes are neutral, but some are significant: even a slight genetic change can produce a new variation in body form, function, or behavior. Variation, both slight and dramatic, is the raw material for natural selection.

Scientists have long been interested in the genealogy of species, that is, in trying to figure out which species are in direct line of descent from which other species. The evolutionary history or "family tree" of an organism (showing how it is related to all other organisms) is called its **phylogeny**. Scientists collect a variety of evidence to construct "phylogenetic diagrams." They compare the physical structures of species living and dead; they seek out information on where living species exist compared to where similar species and fossils are found; and they use various techniques such as **isotopic dating** to identify the ages of different fossils.

Increasingly, they also are using genetics. The ability to decode genetic information has become very sophisticated since the first such efforts were launched in the 1980s. By following the mutation trail in the DNA, scientists have been able to chart ancestral relationships and to estimate the time when various lineages branched off from their forebears.

Another line of evidence used by scientists to construct "phylogenetic diagrams" comes from the field called **evolutionary developmental biology**, referred to informally as evo-devo. This field joins together two approaches: the study of genetic evolution and the studies of how genes control the growth and maturation of individual living organisms. Researchers have found that evolution occurs in large part through inherited changes in the genes that regulate development. Different species may have very similar genomes, but a few differences in regulatory genes, expressed throughout development, cause dramatic differences in appearance and behavior. In embryo and juvenile stages, before the differential gene expression has occurred, similarities between a species and close relatives or ancestors may be more pronounced. This is the explanation for why human embryos exhibit tails and gill-like features at a very early stage of development. It also explains why the juvenile form of a frog is the fish-like tadpole.

The accumulation of evidence about our evolutionary history has led scientists to some fascinating new insights. For example, they now consider birds and crocodiles to be more closely related than lizards and crocodiles, because the first pair shares a more recent common ancestor. The bird line appears to have split off from the crocodile line within the last 200 million years or so, well after the split between lizards and crocodiles. There are many other examples of family trees being redrawn in ways that may seem counter-intuitive to anyone looking only at the external structures of organisms.

Scientists now recognize that two or more species with common traits may *not* necessarily be closely related. An example here involves the horse and the litoptern, a South American hoofed mammal that became extinct more than 10,000 years ago. The litoptern looked much like a modern horse, with four long legs and undivided hooves fit for galloping across plains. Yet the evidence suggests that the horse and the litoptern

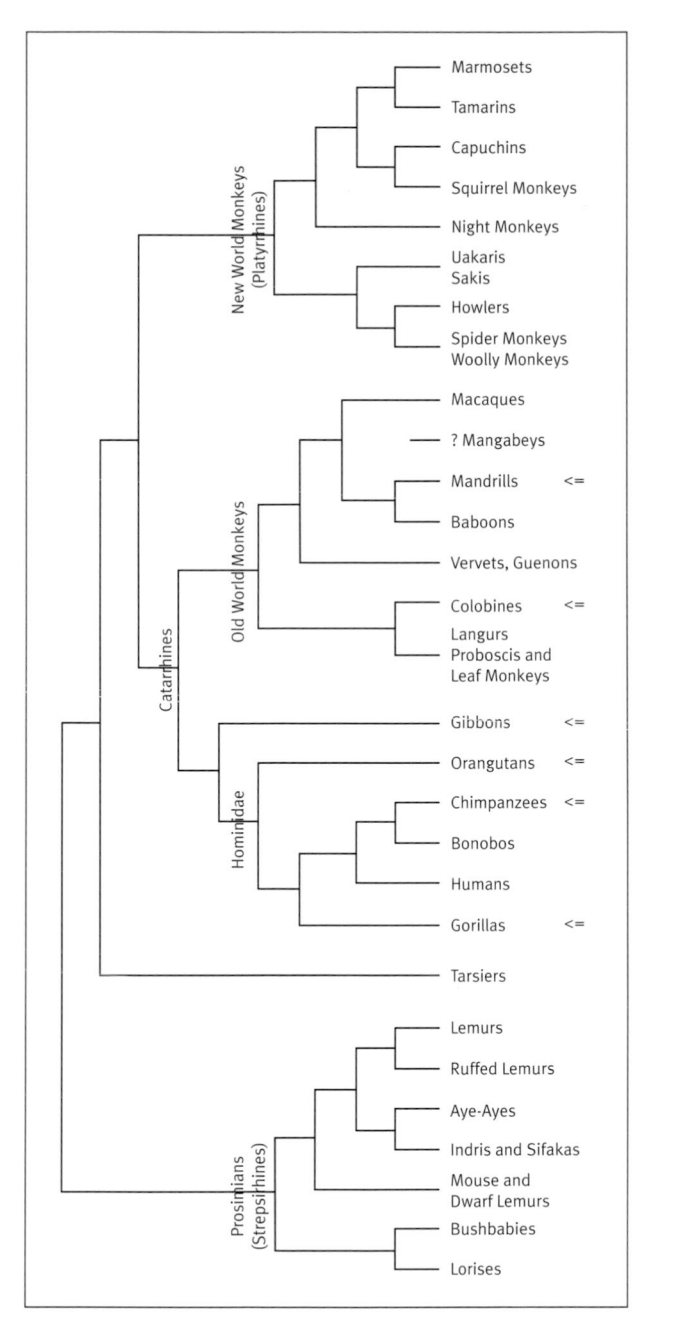

A phylogenetic diagram of primates.

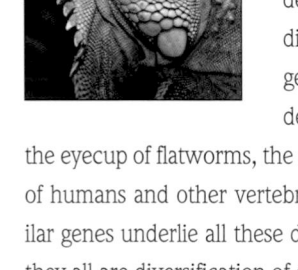

Phylogenetic research reveals that despite their physical similarities, lizards and crocodiles are less closely related than crocodiles and birds.

evolved independently through different lines of descent: the horse evolving in North America and the litoptern separately in South America, millions of years ago when the two continents were disconnected. This is referred to as **convergent evolution**. Scientists have identified many instances where selective pressures in similar ecological circumstances along different lines of descent have resulted in similar biological features.

There are many cases, however, where similar characteristics appear in different species because they *are* linked through a common line of descent. This is what explains the similarities between the bone structure of the wings of bats, the forelimbs of gorillas, and the flippers of whales. Shared characteristics that occur through direct descent are referred to as **homologies**, while similarities due to convergent evolution are called **analogies**.

Scientists do a great deal of detective work to figure out which shared characteristics result from convergent evolution and which from direct descent. Until recently, scientists had believed that different kinds of eyes were the result of convergent evolution. There is incredible variety in eye design, such as the eyespot of microscopic algae, the eyecup of flatworms, the compound eye of dragonflies, and the retinal eye of humans and other vertebrates. However, there is now evidence that similar genes underlie all these different eye designs. One new hypothesis is that they all are diversification of one prototype eye that first emerged in trilobites, small marine animals that were abundant some 540 million years ago. In incremental steps, along various tracks, an abundance of eye types from simple to complex have emerged, each adaptive to its particular niche and all produced through descent with modification from a common ancestor.

Life's origins

The common ancestor to all species found on Earth today was probably not the first creature that ever lived on Earth but merely one situated at a critical fork in the tree of life. The common ancestor itself was probably a descendant of many earlier generations of organisms whose other lines of descent dwindled off into extinction. It was probably no more than a microbe but sufficiently evolved to have a molecular structure that carried hereditary information in the form of DNA.

Prior to the first DNA-based life, scientists believe that there may have been life based on some simpler hereditary mechanism such as RNA. And prior to that, scientists believe, there may have been organic (carbon-containing) molecules formed from the convergence of methane, ammonia, water vapor, hydrogen gases, and other compounds. Such compounds came into existence when the universe already was several billion years old.

The universe itself originated some 13.7 billion years ago, by best estimates, when an infinitesimally small and unimaginably compressed body of matter exploded outward in all directions. The **Big Bang theory** is the predominant explanation in science today for this origin, based on extensive astronomical measurements including evidence that the galaxies are receding from one another. Other pieces of evidence, such as measurements of cosmic background radiation that reflect traces of the explosion, also support this hypothesis.

At first, hydrogen and helium were the predominant elements in the whole universe. Over great amounts of time, swirling clouds of hydrogen coalesced into stars, and the heavier elements were cooked inside these stars through atomic fusion. These elements were scattered across the universe when some of these early stars died in spectacular supernova. About 4–5 billion years ago, some of this matter caught in the sun's gravitational system cohered to form the planet Earth. In its early history, Earth was pelted by solar radiation, meteorites, and comets. Masses of chemicals flowed onto the planet's surface from its own interior in massive eruptions.

The Big Bang, the explosion 13.7 billion years ago of space from an immensely hot and dense state, is the predominant scientific explanation for the origin of the universe.

Out of a billion-year period of violent activity, unimaginable in both its length and intensity, Earth emerged with a gaseous atmosphere and a surface of water and bare rock. It was then that "prebiological" molecules became organized into self-sustaining chemical reactions, kick-started by the infusion of energy from some source such as lightning or heat emanating from the Earth's core. Chemical evolution itself evolved, over some half billion years, into biological evolution.

Origins-of-life researchers now believe that the line between non-life and the first life is not clear-cut. One

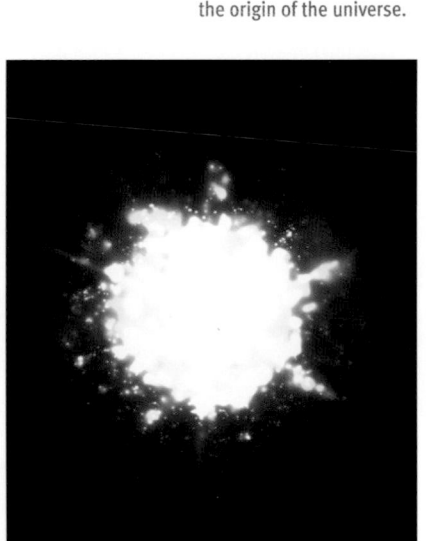

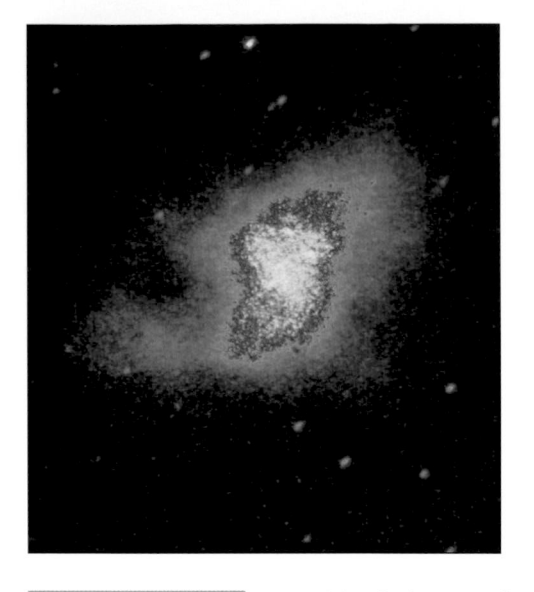

The Crab Nebula is an example of the supernovas that 4–5 billion years ago are thought to have spread the heavier elements into the universe that were eventually caught in the sun's gravitational field and cohered to form the Earth and other planets.

way they define a living thing is by three criteria: it is able to acquire and use energy, it has a membrane that separates itself from its surroundings, and it can reproduce on its own. Under such a definition, the first life forms were ocean-dwelling, single-celled organisms (**prokaryotes**). These appeared between 3.5 and 4 billion years ago. Two main types of prokaryotes eventually evolved: bacteria and archaea.

The arrival of plants and animals

After the evolution of prokaryotes, life stayed in very simple form for about 2 billion years — half of the entire history of life on Earth. Bacteria capable of **photosynthesis** (a means of obtaining energy from the sun) emerged about 3.2 billion years ago, and almost a billion years later — again, a vast and unimaginable span of time — bacteria emerged that produced oxygen as a by-product of photosynthesis. This development was extremely important on two counts. Rising oxygen levels created a poisonous atmosphere that extinguished many species, but others recovered through adaptive mutations to the new atmosphere and flourished. And importantly, the increase in oxygen created the ozone layer. For the first time in Earth's history, its surface was protected from the deadly ultraviolet radiation of the sun. This meant that life finally had the opportunity to evolve up from the water's depths and onto land.

Another significant shift occurred about 2 to 1.5 billion years ago, when there emerged the first organisms (**eukaryotes**) with a nucleus inside their cells and, inside those nuclei, DNA organized into chromosomes. Other specialized features of eukaryotic cells (such as **mitochondria** and **chloroplasts**) probably resulted when distinct single-celled organisms formed symbiotic partnerships (a phenomenon called **endosymbiosis**). Another significant development in the evolution of life occurred around 1 billion years ago, when the first multi-celled animals (called **metazoa**) formed from eukaryotic cells. These included algae and seaweeds and, later, sponges, jellyfish, flat worms, and marine animals known as **arthropods** (animals with an outside or exoskeleton).

The evolution of life in the sea continued through millions of years and into a unique period called the **Cambrian explosion**. This was not an instantaneous event; rather, it was a span of perhaps 30 million years. Still, this is a

Evolution Dialogues

very short time when measured against all of Earth's history. Within the Cambrian period, a great variety of marine life appeared, moved into new habitats, and exhibited new behaviors such as burrowing and active hunting. With one exception, all of the major body plans (**phyla**) of modern animals are first preserved from this era, along with many unusual phyla dissimilar to anything alive today. Scientists hypothesize that many of these life forms had emerged earlier, but during the Cambrian period, they evolved into sizes sufficiently large and skeletons sufficiently hard that they could be preserved as fossils.

This picture of proliferation is complicated by fossil evidence demonstrating that several mass extinctions also occurred during the Cambrian period. One hypothesis, supported by evidence, is that these extinctions were caused by the advancement of glaciers. Indeed, throughout life's history, major geological events have had an enormous and unpredictable effect on evolution: destabilizing some species, extinguishing others, and triggering adaptive changes leading to new species. The continents would merge together, drift apart, and reconnect in new places. Shifting landmasses would break species into separate populations that would then evolve along separate lines. They also would introduce species to new environments and new competitors, which would have an effect on which mutations would be adaptive in their descendents.

Massive volcanic eruptions would fill the sky with ash and spew forth molten lava that would blanket vast regions and create new land and merge continents together. Meteors would collide with the Earth, creating massive havoc around their points of impact and, in some cases, global disruption. Climates would undergo massive reversals between warm and cold and wet and dry. Such events would destroy and transform environments and create new niches to be filled. The evolution of life would move persistently through all these events.

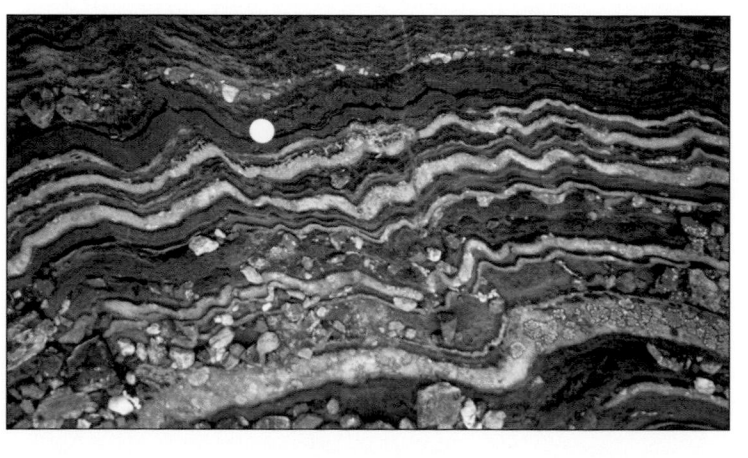

Photo: ©David C. Greene, Denison University

Rocks of the Isua sequence in southwest Greenland are greater than 3.7 billion years old. Chemical signatures left in the rocks are the earliest discovered evidence of life, predating all fossils. These signatures are traces of the carbon that is (along with oxygen) a by-product of bacterial photosynthesis.

Geological upheavals, including volcanic eruptions and meteor collisions, have had enormous environmental and so evolutionary impact.

About 500 million years ago, the first animals with spines (**vertebrates**) evolved; these were the earliest forms of fish. Life flourished in seas and lakes for millions of years before spreading onto land, first as bacteria living on rock, then as bacteria living in soil created by the decomposition of previous generations of bacteria. As soil built up, simple plants and fungi emerged. One lineage of arthropods also began to populate the land and diversified into millipedes, centipedes, spiders, and insects.

Fish that had muscular, or lobed, fins and a lung-like capacity to obtain oxygen from air as well as water were able to seek food along shorelines as well as in the water. Out of this lineage of "mud skippers," other species emerged in which the fins operated in a leg-like fashion. Called **tetrapods**, some of these lineages further evolved into **amphibians** — vertebrate animals that as juveniles breathe through gills and live in the water and as adults typically live on land and breathe through lungs.

Another lineage of tetrapods evolved into reptiles and, around 230 million years ago, one of the reptilian lineages gave rise to dinosaurs. Some species descended through this line grew to gigantic proportions. The first mammals diverged from a line of reptiles and remained small. Birds also branched out of the dinosaur lineage, and some of these also were a great deal larger than their kind today.

Plants evolved to bear seeds and this enabled them to spread more rapidly. The land became covered with ferns, mosses, horsetails, cycads (palm-like plants) and, later, conifers. Some insects evolved the ability to fly — one ancient dragonfly had a wingspan of two feet.

Around 130 million years ago, the first flowering plants evolved. Birds and insects were attracted to the flowers for nourishment and helped spread the pollen and seeds, enabling plants to spread even faster across the land. These interactions contributed to the diversification of both flowers and plants and their pollinators.

Around 65 million years ago, in yet another major extinction event to beset the Earth, the dinosaurs died out. Birds and mammals survived whatever cataclysmic event or events that had altered the environment so drastically as to kill off the largest beasts of the land. Over the span of millions more years, these remaining populations recovered, diversified, and became abundant. Some lines of mammal species evolved back toward the water, and from these lineages came whales, dolphins, and seals. A few lines of mammal species evolved toward flight, and this produced bats and flying squirrels. A group of tree-dwelling mammals branched into the line of **primates**. The direct ancestors of today's lemurs and monkeys existed by 40 million years ago. Grasslands emerged, as did horses, other hoofed mammals, and canines.

Human origins

Researchers of human evolution are called **paleoanthropologists**. These scientists look for fossils of species that are closely related to *Homo sapiens*, the scientific name given to the modern human species. They analyze early human fossil remains, for example, by reconstructing skeletons from bits of fossilized bone and comparing the resulting anatomy to other reconstructed

The evolution of seeds enabled plants to spread rapidly and diversify into ferns, mosses, horsetails, cycads, and, later, conifers.

skeletons or by scanning bones to peer into their interior structure. They also study the material products of early human existence such as the tools, paintings, carvings, burials, fire rings, and other artifacts left behind by our ancestors. Paleoanthropologists conduct chemical analysis of bones that reveals information about diet and other biochemical factors. They also extract and analyze DNA samples from ancient bones to compare with the DNA of modern humans, chimpanzees, and other primates.

The history of human origins is still sketchy, but scientists agree on the broad outlines. Sometime between 5 to 8 million years ago, there was a major fork in the branching evolution of primate species. The chimpanzee lineage (which includes two living species, the chimpanzee and bonobo) evolved from one set of branches. Modern humans evolved out of the other. Species that fit onto this second set of branches are referred to as **hominins**.

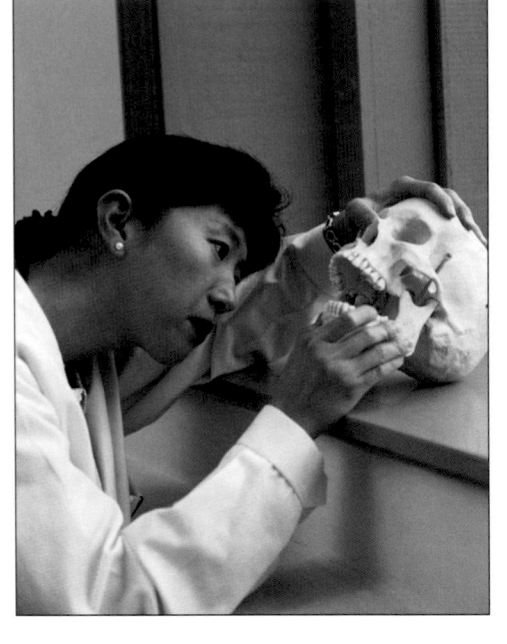

The study of human evolution includes the comparison of early and modern hominid remains.

Thousands of hominin fossils have been discovered in Africa, Europe, and Asia. Most of the finds have been of a few bones or teeth or skull fragments. However, in some instances a whole skull or a number of bones together have been discovered. There also are cases where a significant portion of a whole skeleton has been unearthed.

Yet, even a fragment can reveal a lot. A section of pelvis can indicate whether the individual was bipedal like a human or a forward-tilting "knuckle-walker" like a chimpanzee. A leg bone can reveal the creature's probable height and weight. A skull and the signature of its muscle attachments will indicate brain size and can offer hints about intellectual capacity and speaking ability. The skull also provides clues as to mobility. There is a hole in the skull through which the spinal cord passes. This hole is toward the back in species that lean forward when walking, but it is toward the bottom for species that walk upright.

Lined up in a continuum from earliest to most recent as determined by various dating methods, the fossils of early hominins conform to an overall trend toward larger brains and bodies, smaller teeth, and more slender and upright physiques. Archaeological evidence also suggests that behavior changed over time. For example, projectile points found near later fossil hominin species indicate those individuals made spears, consistent with increased reliance on tools for survival. Yet each fossil species bears its own combination of non-human and modern human characteristics, and there is no single, clear line of progression.

One reason for this non-linearity is that many of the discovered fossils are of hominin species that became extinct — that died out and left no descendants. They evolved down separate, somewhat parallel branches to the human line but were not our direct ancestors. Metaphorically speaking, their relationships to surviving humans are like that of spinster aunts and bachelor uncles — all childless and deceased. Our species is the only surviving branch among numerous members of the hominin family that evolved in the last few million years.

Like the dividing line between non-life and life, there appears to be no clear point at which pre-humans evolved into humans. Many of the oldest quasi-human fossils have been grouped into a **genus** called *Australop-*

ithecus, but in the past decade or so, fossils have been discovered that appear to be even older and more primitive than *Australopithecus* and yet are not quite like chimpanzees or any other of the great apes.

The earliest species that is tentatively placed in the lineage leading to modern humans is dubbed *Homo habilis*, which translates as "handyman." The name comes from the fact that stones used as tools have been found near fossil remains of *Homo habilis*. The earliest *Homo habilis* fossils are dated to about 2.4 million years ago. Members of this species appear to have been small relative to modern humans. They had ape-like skeletons, with arms nearly as long as their legs. Yet overall, their skeletons were decidedly human-like, with the pelvis and legs and spine not like anything seen in apes. *Homo habilis*, like *Australopithecus* before it, is a clear example of a transitional species between early primate and modern human.

The first several million years of human history took place entirely within the continent that is now Africa. But by 1.8 million years ago, some populations began to migrate outward. Fossils that have been classified into a species named *Homo erectus* have been found both within Africa and as far away as China and Java. *Homo erectus* had a relatively upright posture, with long, straight legs that allowed for efficient walking.

Homo erectus was taller and larger than species that lived earlier and had a larger brain, though not as large as modern humans. It had a thick skull with a prominent brow ridge, a low sloping forehead, and no chin, but compared to earlier hominins, its face protruded less and had smaller teeth. Fossils show this species to have existed for more than 1.5 million years, finally dwindling down to some remnant tribes in Asia before dying out, possibly as recently as 40,000 years ago.

From populations that had migrated out of Africa, another major group evolved, and this was *Homo neanderthalensis*. Populations of this species first emerged in Europe and West Asia more than 200,000 years ago from earlier hominins that had wandered in those directions. A great many Neanderthal fossils have been recovered, and their analysis indicates that they are not ancestors of humans, but rather another line of hominins that overlapped in time with early modern *Homo sapiens*. They did not look radically different from humans. On average they were stockier, with big bones and big joints, and they did have a different skull shape. They had a long and low braincase that sat immediately behind a largish face with a deep brow jutting out over their eyes, a large nasal opening, and a receding chin.

The Neanderthals lived during periods of extreme climate change and must have been highly adaptable. They were apparently hunter-gatherers who were able to kill big game through ambush hunting. Bone chemistry confirms that they were carnivores. Based on anthropological evidence, they are believed to have moved about in small groups from one rough campsite to the next, without permanent settlement. They had sophisticated stone tools and primitive spears but neither great variety nor artistic adornment to their objects. Many had brains larger than those of living humans, although their bulky, muscular bodies probably required a larger distribution of nerves compared to modern human bodies. The inside of their skulls suggest that their brains were shaped like those of modern humans. Among other things, this indicates possible language capacity. There is debate among scientists about whether the anatomy of their skulls, throat, and spinal cords suggest a capacity for oral speech at the level of modern humans. Neanderthals are the earliest hominins known to bury their dead. Recovered bones that show sign of crippling injuries suggest that Neanderthals also cared for their sick and injured.

Homo sapiens first emerged in Africa around 200,000 years ago. Neanderthals and *Homo sapiens* both moved in and out of the Middle East for many thousands of years. The distinct behaviors of modern humans appeared gradually within Africa: hafted bone spear points appeared around 90,000 years ago, beads for personal ornamentation around 40,000–50,000 years ago, and artistic paintings around 40,000 years ago. The *Homo sapiens* populations that moved into Europe some 40,000 years ago had a novel ability to make symbolic artifacts. This set them apart from their Neanderthal neighbors, who from evidence left behind do not seem to have advanced far in terms of cultural activity.

Early modern humans in Europe, called "Cro-Magnons" after the region in France where the first remains were found, left behind jewelry and tools with carved decorations. They made paintings on cave walls, had simple musical instruments, and probably sang and danced. They buried their dead with beautiful grave goods and beaded garments. They used bone needles to fashion clothing and simple kilns to bake ceramic figures. They made stone tools of greater variety and sophistication and from bones and antlers as

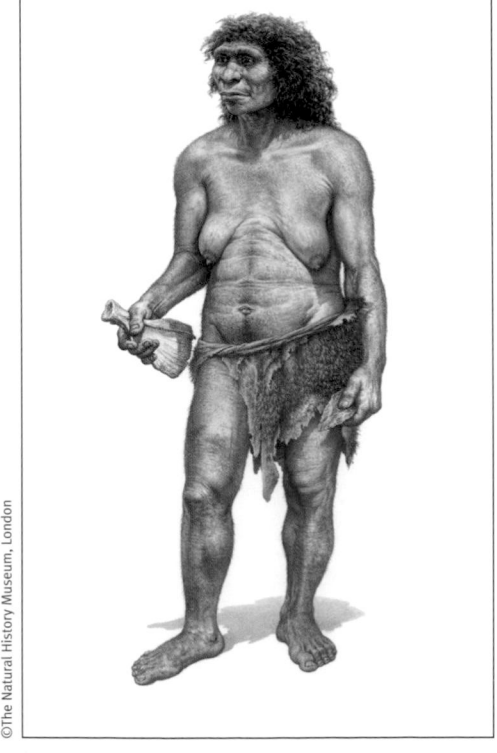

Neanderthals (shown in an artist's depiction) cohabited the Earth with *Homo sapiens* until about 30,000 years ago. It is unclear why they became extinct.

©The Natural History Museum, London

well as stone. They had acquired the ability to reason symbolically and to be inventive and creative. Such abilities may have been connected with their acquisition of language: language permits information to be transmitted between generations so that technologies could be elaborated upon rather than reinvented.

Symbolic culture appears to have been the ultimate advantage. After moving into Europe and West Asia, *Homo sapiens* completely displaced the Neanderthals. How this occurred is unknown. Possibly, the Neanderthals died out in violent conflict with the newly arriving *Homo sapiens*. Possibly they were absorbed by interbreeding with the newcomers, though whether this was physiologically feasible is a matter of debate among scientists given the current evidence. Another possibility is that they simply lost out in the competition for resources. Whatever the process, *Homo sapiens* came to dominate the planet as the exclusive surviving hominin species.

Even as humans emerged, other lineages of plants and animals continued to diversify and evolve — just as they continue to do into the present time. The most prominent witnesses to evolution in today's world are the rapidly evolving diseases such as HIV and tuberculosis, which through exposure to antibiotic medicines are facing selective pressures that cause resistant forms to survive. Other species may not evolve as quickly as bacteria, but no species is static. With each generation within every living species, variation is introduced and selection pressures are at work to shape the traits that are inherited and passed on to the next generation.

The vast amount of time over which the evolution of life on our planet has occurred can be extremely hard to conceptualize. Sometimes it helps to use analogies that are closer to everyday experience. The appendix to this volume (p. 199) provides several such examples.

The future of evolution

There are two insights that can be gleaned from the story of evolution. One is that humans evolved very late in the grand scheme of biological evolution: our species is one tiny, recently emerged twig in a vast and dense thicket of life. The other insight is that, of all the millions and millions of species that have ever existed on Earth, humans stand apart. In the 4 billion years of life's history, *Homo sapiens* is the only animal that has acquired symbolic behaviors such as language and art. Distinct from other species, humans operate within the framework of **cultural evolution**.

Culture is defined as socially transmitted behavior patterns, beliefs, institutions, and all other products of human work and thought. The evolution of culture is **Lamarckian** in the sense that what a person acquires in his or her lifetime *can* be passed on to the next generation. Through the acquisition, preservation, and transmission of knowledge, humans have been able to readjust the environment so that it is, on its own, less selective. To give but one simple example: we build dams, which allow us to live on previously flooded ground and to generate electricity, which in turn allows us to see in the dark, use electrical tools to build strong homes that protect us from predators, cook and cool our food, and stay warm at night.

The pace of cultural evolution has quickened in our lifetimes. We can now design drugs that give us significant control over our health, behavior, and emotions. Through chemicals, transplants, and genetic engineering, we can prolong life, increase our intellectual capacities and athletic performance, and change our appearance. Reproductive techniques allow parents to select characteristics of their children such as gender and freedom from inherited disorders. Through the Internet, we share information and work collectively in ways never before imagined.

All such cultural behaviors, taken together, could have a significant effect on who survives to reproduce, and this affects the gene pool of descendants. We are creating what has been described as a post-human future — a world in which we maximize our ability to modify ourselves. Humans continue to evolve, but not exclusively through the "trial and error" and long-term mechanisms of biological evolution.

The development of drugs that influence our health, behavior, or emotions represents a form of cultural evolution that bears on our biological evolution.

At the same time, humans have unprecedented effects on the continued existence of other forms of life on the planet. Scientists have identified five major extinction periods in the world's history, and many believe that we are now entering another period of mass dying. "The Sixth Great Extinction," as it is called, could rival any that has occurred in the past. Thousands of species are disappearing each year; the average extinction rate is esti-

mated to be 1,000–10,000 times faster than at any point in the past 60 million years. For the first time in human history, existing species are lost at a faster rate than new species are evolving.

The contributing factors to this accelerated rate of extinction are all human-caused: the degradation and destruction of natural habitats, the over-hunting and over-harvesting of species, and the deliberate and accidental transport of exotic species into new territories where they out-compete and displace native species. In addi-

146   **Evolution Dialogues**

tion, native species are threatened by genetically engineered organisms that cross-cultivate when they migrate into the wild. And, of course, climate change brought about by industrial development is altering the environment in ways that many species may not be able to endure. Widespread extinction of key species can have cascading effects, altering entire ecosystems and perhaps threatening the survival of humankind itself.

Life on Earth has been resilient. The human-stimulated extinction of vast numbers of species and even humans ourselves would not likely be the end of the evolution of life on Earth. Yet if evolutionary history is our guide, the balance of life that follows a mass extinction takes millions of years to emerge and is vastly different from what preceded it.

Many scientists believe that a tragic Sixth Extinction is still avoidable. According to the Earth Policy Institute, "While this may be the first time in history that a single species can precipitate a mass extinction event, it is also the first time in history that a single species can act to prevent it."[27] Humans increasingly have the scientific understanding to live harmoniously with the other species of the Earth. They may, however, need something beyond science to find the vision and will to do so.

Perhaps the single most significant factor contributing to the "Sixth Great Extinction" is human-induced degradation or destruction of habitat.

FURTHER READING

Benchmarks for Science Literacy, AAAS (Oxford University Press, 1993)

Evolution: The triumph of an idea, Carl Zimmer (Harper Perennial, 2002)

Human Evolution: A very short introduction, Bernard Wood (Oxford University Press, 2005)

The Human Odyssey: Four million years of human evolution, Ian Tattersall (iUniverse, 2001)

Science for All Americans, F. James Rutherford and Andrew Ahlgren; AAAS (Oxford University Press, 1990)

Contemporary stances toward evolution

Angela Rawlett stepped into the foyer of the campus ministry building just as her religious advisor Phil Compton was stepping out of his office. In one hand he held a coffee mug. With the other, he held open the door for two people coming behind him. An attractive woman wearing a headscarf was followed by an intense-looking older gentleman in a dark suit.

Phil smiled when he saw his student. "How nice that you happened to come by just now," he said. "I would like you to meet Dr. Fatima Ibrahim and Rabbi Jacob Weiner. They are partnering with me for next fall's senior seminar."

Angela shook hands with the two visitors. "Will you be a senior next year, Angela?" Dr. Ibrahim asked. "No," the student answered. "I'll just be a sophomore."

"What a terrible shame!" Rabbi Weiner exclaimed. "You won't be able to join our seminar. Perhaps we could make an exception?" He turned to Phil. Angela could not tell if he was serious or joking.

"It may not interest her," responded Phil.

"What's your topic?" asked Angela.

"The official title is 'Peoples of the Book: Points of Divergence and Convergence,'" said Phil. "Basically, it's the intermural version of my spring seminar on doctrinal differences."

"Will it be sort of a debate class?" asked Angela.

"Not at all," said Dr. Ibrahim. "It is a dialogue. We will talk about what we have in common. Where we disagree, we will keep talking."

"There will be debate," said Rabbi Weiner.

"If history is our guide, there may be some heated exchanges," Phil said, adopting a conciliatory tone. "But that's assuming we have students of all three faiths registered in the course. We could end up with a conclave of Lutherans if we don't get this campus exchange going."

"Yes, I'll work on that at my end," noted the rabbi. "But even if we had a roomful of Presbyterians, you would have your heated exchanges."

Phil smiled in acknowledgement. He turned to Angela. "What brings you by?"

The student blushed slightly. "I didn't mean to interrupt you. I wanted to drop off a flier about something the biology department is sponsoring next week. Since you might be interested." She offered Phil a sheet of blue paper. He moved his coffee cup to his left hand so that he could accept the paper with his right.

"'The Evolution of Life Elsewhere,'" Phil read aloud. "Sounds intriguingly speculative."

"Evolution," said Dr. Ibrahim, turning to the minister. "Now there's a topic that raises more fireworks in your community than it does in mine."

"Or mine," said Rabbi Weiner.

"Why is that?" asked Angela.

"The science does not conflict with our parable of creation," explained Dr. Ibrahim.

The rabbi nodded his head. "Likewise. To the extent that the science helps inform interpretation of our sacred stories, we welcome it."

"There is a strain within the Christian tradition that strives toward certainty," added Phil. "Certainty demands literalism. Evolutionary

Evolution Dialogues

theory and literal constructions of Genesis are what make the fireworks."

"Evolution science raises new questions with every new finding," the Muslim professor noted. "That's how science works. Every scientific discovery begets new scientific questions and at the same time provokes new conceptualizations of our religious texts."

"I suppose some people find that spiritually energizing," said Angela. "But it can be very disturbing."

"What we all have in common," interjected Dr. Ibrahim, "is that we are all seekers of the truth. Evolutionary theory does not fit the truth as it has been revealed to some people. Or at least, it does not seem to them to fit."

"It can be an ill-sized shoe, even for me," said Rabbi Weiner. "It's as real as leather, I know that, but it sometimes rubs against my heel."

As Angela puzzled over that remark, the two visitors said their good-byes and departed.

"He may word things a bit unusually," said Phil, "but Jacob's quite brilliant. And he's unusually generous. When I had to leave town for three weeks to tend to my dying father, he took in my cat. Later I found out he is allergic to animals."

"Why would he do that?" asked Angela.

"He happened to stop by my office just after I received the phone call about my father's stroke," Phil explained. "I was in a mad rush to make arrangements. I believe he offered impulsively."

"But why would he do that?" Angela asked again. "Why do people do things against their own self-interest?"

"Altruism," answered Phil.

"Isn't that a circular answer?" responded the student.

"You're quick today," Phil said, smiling a little. "We define altruism as instinctive cooperative behavior that is detrimental to the individual but increases the fitness of other members of the species. So we could rephrase your question as, why did Jacob care for my cat, thereby forgoing his own fitness?"

"Maybe it wasn't to his benefit," said Angela, "but the urge to assist may have evolved in human beings through centuries of living together in communities."

"So then the question is, how did this trait first come about? Why did the Neanderthal, a hundred thousands years ago, take care of their injured instead of abandoning them?"

"Maybe the injured person was very wise," the student offered. "Or maybe helping the injured is a kind of insurance, against the day when you get injured yourself."

Credit: NASA

Artist's concept
showing the newly
discovered Neptune-
sized extrasolar
planet circling the
star Gliese 436.

Phil scratched the side of his head pensively with the edge of the flier. "I have an idea. Perhaps you should take a philosophy class next fall. 'Thinking About Values.' That's what they call the intro course. It covers virtue, doing good, duty, and meaningful existence. Vice and evil, too."

"I can see why you recommend that," said Angela. "I don't think science alone could ever answer my question about what makes the rabbi a good man. Anyway, I'd better get moving."

"Before you go, tell me a bit more about this 'Evolution of Life Elsewhere' program," Phil said.

"Dr. Brown — that's my biology professor — he was explaining how astronomers have discovered more than 150 planets outside our solar system."

"But could any of those planets support life?" asked the minister. "If I recall what I have read, most of them are just gaseous giants."

"Professor Brown says they've discovered a planet in the constellation Aquarius that's only seven times larger than ours," Angela answered. "He says it's only a matter of time before they find Earth-like planets that could be habitable."

"So this is a discussion of what conditions are needed for life to evolve, and where we might find them?"

"Yes, I think so. But from the speakers' list, it looks like they'll also be talking about implications."

"Implications?"

"The kinds of questions I've been asking you all this year, except times ten," said Angela. "Like, what does it mean for humans if there is intelligent life in another galaxy? What do you think about that? Do you think it would mean that Jesus Christ has been to their planet?"

"What an odd picture that draws in the mind," said Phil.

"No kidding," Angela answered. "The study of evolution keeps drawing bigger and bigger question marks next to the word God in my brain. But I don't mind that anymore. I kind of like the thinking that the questions make me do."

CHAPTER 8

Contemporary stances toward evolution

A touchy subject

Lisa Westberg Peters is a Minnesota writer who has authored more than a dozen children's books. Many of her works are about nature, such as *The Sun, The Wind, and The Rain* and *Earthshake: Poems from the Ground Up.* For many years, Peters has been invited into school classrooms to teach children about the writing process, using as examples passages from her own books.

But three times in recent years, she has been asked to not make any reference to one book she has written. That text, which received a Minnesota Book Award for children's nonfiction in 2004, is called *Our Family Tree.*

Linda Westberg Peters, the author of *Our Family Tree*, was surprised to discover that her children's book exploring evolution has been seen by some as controversial.

"All of us are part of an old, old family," the book begins. "The roots of our family tree reach way back to the beginning of life on earth. We've changed a lot since then." Accompanied by beautiful color illustrations, *Our Family Tree* explains how humans inherited their DNA from the earliest one-celled life forms, their backbones from early fish, their legs and feet from early amphibians, their fingernails from primates, and their large brains from early humans. It concludes that people today have three and a half billion years' worth of ancestors and are related one way or another to all living things. In poetic language, the content supports Minnesota state science standards. These expect elementary students to understand that biological populations change over time and that many species that once lived on earth are now extinct.

"It's a cute book," a newspaper article quoted a principal as saying. He heads one of the schools where Peters' book was not welcome. "There's nothing wrong with it. We just don't need that kind of debate."[28]

This textbook contains material on evolution. Evolution is a theory, not a fact, regarding the origin of living things. This material should be approached with an open mind, studied carefully, and critically considered.

In 2002, the Cobb County, Georgia School Board required that these stickers be placed on biology textbooks. They were subsequently declared unconstitutional by a federal judge, and the case was appealed.

The debate he was referring to is the one over evolution. The reluctance of a few Minnesota schools to even incidentally expose schoolchildren to a book on the theme of common descent as articulated by Charles Darwin (1809–1882) speaks to the widespread public unease over evolution. Despite the vast accumulation of scientific evidence in support of the theory, despite the overwhelming consensus of scientists that evolution has occurred and that Darwin's theory provides the best basic explanation of how biological change has occurred over time on this planet, and despite the keystone role the theory plays in guiding contemporary scientific exploration, it makes many people distressed and even outraged.

This discomfort has translated into efforts across the country to eliminate or undermine the teaching of evolution. Several school boards and state legislatures have proposed and in some places passed resolutions requiring that biology textbooks be modified with stickers disclaiming evolution as "a theory, not a fact." In other states, proposals have been considered or adopted that require teachers to read a disclaimer about evolution before teaching the subject. Another approach has been to write into the biology curriculum the teaching of so-called "alternative theories to evolution" or the alleged "controversy" over evolution or "evidence for and against" evolution. Yet another strategy has been to remove evolution from teaching standards, which in effect removes it from the classroom. Another is to alter the definition of science so that supernatural causes might be included within its explanations of nature.

All across the country, school boards, education policy-makers, legislators, teachers, parents, and of course students are caught up in various debates over whether and how evolution should be taught. Even in places where the discord has not yet extended, the teaching of evolution has been suppressed by the fear of stirring up controversy. With class time a limited resource, teachers tend to skip over evolution and focus instead on less disturbing science topics.

Most of the challengers to evolution are religiously motivated Christians. At the same time, many religiously motivated people have sought to constructively relate their beliefs with the science of evolution. As there was in Darwin's time, there is today a spectrum of views on how religious faith and science can be related. The continuum ranges from those who would

Evolution Dialogues

change science in order to make it consistent with their theological commitments to those who would modify their religious understanding in order to take account of an evolving universe. In the middle are those who have tried to avoid any challenge by separating evolution and religion into distinctive domains.

The theory of evolution describes how all life forms on the Earth are historically related to each other and change over time.

In any review of society's response to evolution, it helps to keep in mind what the theory is about. In brief, evolution proposes that the forms of life that populate the Earth have changed over time and continue to change. Furthermore, the theory holds that all species living and extinct are related to each other. From a common ancestor almost 4 billion years ago, the great diversity of life has emerged. Charles Darwin called this process "descent with modification."

There are two primary features of this process. First, there is variation among offspring: children are different from their parents and from one another. Second, there is the mechanism of **natural selection**. By virtue of this mechanism, in any population where organisms vary in their inherited traits and where more are born than can possibly survive, on average, the offspring that are better adapted to the local environment are the ones that tend to survive and to reproduce and so pass their traits on to the next generation.

It should be remembered that evolution is a *scientific* theory. A scientific theory is an explanation of processes or structures in nature well supported by observations or experiments. A basic ground rule that has allowed scientific discovery to flourish is that scientific explanations must be based only on evidence obtained in the natural world. Explanations that rely on non-natural or supernatural causes do not fall into the domain of science.

One of the questions that scientists have sought to answer is how the diversity of life can be explained as the effect of natural causes. Based on evidence that scientists have amassed over centuries from many different fields of study, it has been found that the diversity of life is explained well by the theory of biological evolution. However, the theory is subject to refinement and no absolute certainty can ever be achieved. A scientific theory can never be proved to be certain. It is either supported or challenged by relevant evidence from nature.

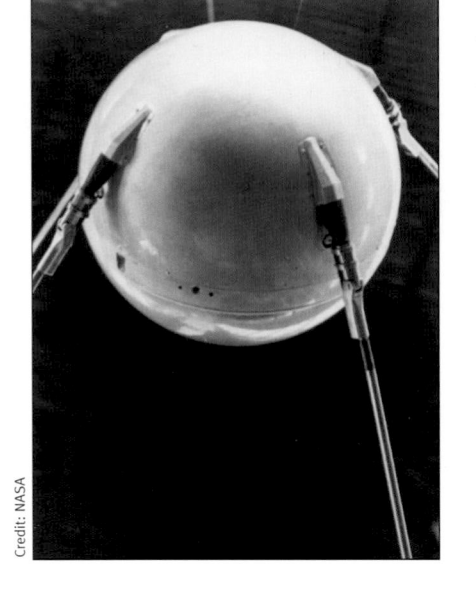

Credit: NASA

In 1957, the former Soviet Union launched the first satellite, Sputnik.

"Scientific" creationism

What precipitated the various challenges to evolution that have emerged over the past 50 years was not something on Earth but something in space. In 1957, Russia launched the first satellite, Sputnik. Americans were distraught at the idea of losing a "space race" to the Soviet Union. This event ignited an educational firestorm in the United States. Public attention focused on the state of American science and on American science education in particular.

One outcome of this national soul-searching was the publication of a federally subsidized biology textbook series in which evolution was the central unifying concept. Commercial publishers soon followed suit. Evolution had virtually dropped out of textbooks and the classroom in the years following the Scopes Trial of 1925, which had centered on a Tennessee law prohibiting its teaching. Now with evolution back in the curriculum in a prominent way, the campaign against it was reignited.

Another event at about the same time added momentum to anti-evolution efforts. This was the 1961 publication of *The Genesis Flood* by Henry Morris (1918–2006), a hydraulic engineer, and John C. Whitcomb, Jr. (1925–), a **fundamentalist Christian** theologian. The book proposed that there was scientific support for the idea that the Earth was less than 10,000 years old and that it and its animal and human inhabitants had been created by God in a literal six-day period. While such ideas were not new, they were generally rare among 20th century Christians and held largely by members of small sectarian denominations such as the Seventh-Day Adventists.

In their book, Morris and Whitcomb proposed that the existence of fossils and geological formations such as the Grand Canyon could be explained by one great worldwide event. This, they claimed, was the flood of Noah as described in the book of Genesis and it happened just a few thousand years ago. This position came to be known as **flood geology** or **young-Earth creationism**. Morris went on to assist with the founding of the Creation Research Society in 1963 and the Institute for Creation Research in 1972. Both of these organizations, which still exist, aggressively promoted the young-earth idea.

Although young-Earth creationists succeeded in bringing many fundamentalist Christians into their camp, there were other conservative Christians who remained persuaded by the evidence that the Earth was very old. Such people tended to believe that each creation day in the Genesis account represented a long epoch of time but that humans, nevertheless, had been created specially by God relatively recently (this is called the **day-age theory**). Others believed that God created the heavens and Earth and then after a large span of time recreated the world in six days (this is called the **gap theory**). Old-Earth and young-Earth creationists disagreed on the details of the timing of creation, but what they had in common was **special creation** — the belief that God had created each kind of creature, including and especially humans, separately from all others. It is this conviction about the direct divine creation of individual kinds that is generally called **creationism**.

Christian fundamentalists in the 1960s who opposed evolution were much more organized than their counterparts had been in the 1920s. Their movement had grown substantially and now had its own radio stations, churches, and Bible institutes. But in the first half of the 20th century, science in the United States itself had become a more powerful cultural force and commanded great respect. Many of the leading evolutionary biologists were located in the United States. Those promoting evolution obtained judicial advantage when the U.S. Supreme Court ruled in 1968 that it was unlawful to ban the teaching of evolution simply because it conflicted with certain religious views. Such bans were found to be a violation of the constitutional protection against the establishment of a religion by the government.

In response, those who wanted creationism taught in public schools recast their defense into advocacy for what they now called **"scientific" creationism**. The book by Morris and Whitcomb became the foundational work for this effort. Supposedly scientific claims were made to support creationist doctrine. Among these were the claim that the fossil record did not support the hypothesis that new species emerged out of lineages of older species; that the standard methods for determining the planet's age (such as **isotopic dating**) were faulty; that there was not sufficient time for evolution to have occurred; and that each species, especially humans, could be shown to have an independent origin. All of these claims were quickly rebutted by scientists either as erroneous on their face or as distortions of genuine science.

Nevertheless, advocates of "scientific" creationism lobbied for its inclusion in the public school

The Supreme Court ruled against banning the teaching of evolution in public schools in 1968 and against teaching "scientific" creationism in 1987.

science curriculum, calling for "equal time" or "balanced treatment," as if it were a valid scientific alternative to evolution. Urged on by a grassroots campaign, by 1977 more than 20 state legislatures were considering bills that would require instruction in "scientific" creationism whenever evolutionary biology was taught.

Arkansas became the center of the controversy when, in 1981, it became the first state to pass an equal time bill. The American Civil Liberties Union through its Arkansas state branch again challenged the law as it had the Tennessee anti-evolution law in the 1925 Scopes trial. This time, there was a long list of religious leaders and science organizations as well as local parents of schoolchildren as plaintiffs, with the lead plaintiff being a Presbyterian minister.

The trial took place in a federal district court and the judge's decision overturned the Arkansas law. The state of Arkansas did not appeal the decision but a similar law in Louisiana was argued all the way up to the Supreme Court. In 1987, the high court found that "scientific" creationism was in fact a religious position, not science, and that to require its teaching was a violation of the Constitutional separation of church and state. Therefore, the court concluded, "scientific" creationism could not be taught in the public science classroom.

The 1987 Supreme Court ruling against "scientific" creationism also allowed that alternatives to evolution could be taught in public schools if they were legitimately scientific. Proponents of "intelligent design" claim that ID is science, although there is no actual research to support this claim.

"Intelligent Design"

By the 1990s, it had become clear that the courts would not permit religious doctrine, even if clothed in science-like language, to dictate science classroom content. Yet it also had become evident that there were no legal obstacles to teaching alternative *scientific* theories to evolution, if any could be found. Accordingly, some of those who objected to evolution on religious grounds dropped the term "creationism" from their vocabulary. They began to avoid any explicitly religious references and to couch their arguments in increasingly scholarly and scientific language. They also reemphasized their focus on state and local school boards rather than legislatures.

What emerged was a position that has come to be known as **"intelligent design,"** often referred to by the shorthand reference "ID." It first appeared in a 1984 book called *The Mystery of Life's Origins,* written collectively by a chemist, an engineer, and a geochemist. The authors argued that the emergence of the first living things and many other biological phenomena had not yet been explained by science and, more importantly, never could be. The book mentioned briefly the notion that there must have been some intelligence (not named or described) involved in the origin of life. This was basically a revival of the **God of the Gaps** position: the idea that what could not be explained by natural means (the "gaps") constituted evidence of a supernatural hand at work.

A Christian organization called the Foundation for Thought and Ethics that spearheaded the publication of *The Mystery of Life's Origins* also published another book, *Of Pandas and People,* in 1989. It was offered as a supplemental biology textbook and was devoted to the argument that there is scientific evidence disproving Darwinian evolution. *Of Pandas and People* also gave considerable space to "intelligent design" and offered a lengthy defense of it.

Although *Of Pandas and People* was adopted by school systems in a couple of states, the book that really put "intelligent design" before the American public was *Darwin on Trial,* written by Phillip Johnson (1940–), a University of California at Berkeley law professor. Johnson had been inspired to write his 1991 book because he was frustrated by presentations of Darwin's theory that seemed to relish in the exclusion of God from explanations of natural phenomena. He was offended by the claims of some scientists that their naturalistic explanations made belief in God incredible. Approaching evolutionary theory as a lawyer, he thought he saw holes in the case for evolution. Furthermore, he was convinced that evolution only survived as the predominant explanation for biological history because, in his view, it supported an atheistic, materialist philosophy that pervaded modern culture.

Previously published anti-evolution writings had for the most part been ignored by scientists. However, because Johnson was a tenured professor at a respected public university, his book was reviewed by a few scientists in prominent journals. Though these reviews were highly critical of Johnson's arguments, they were noticed by mainstream journalists, and the new dispute over evolution was soon brought to the attention of the general public.

Shortly thereafter, works supporting ID were published by two of its major proponents. The first was an article published in 1996 in *The Princeton Theological Review* entitled "What Every Theologian Should Know About Creation, Evolution, and Design" by William Dembski (1960–),

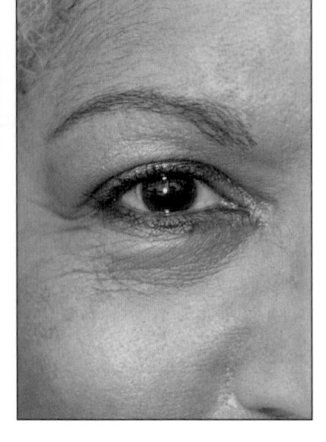

William Paley, in the early 1800s, compared the complexity of a watch to that of the human eye and concluded that each implied a "designer."

a theologically trained mathematician and philosopher. The second published later in the same year was *Darwin's Black Box* by Michael Behe (1952–), a biochemist.

The ID argument involves two primary claims. The first, developed by Dembski, is that phenomena have only three possible causes: natural law, chance, or intelligent agency. If a phenomenon cannot be the result of the first two, it must be an expression of "intelligent design." Dembski has proposed a mathematically inspired form of analysis that he claims can unerringly identify "**complex specified information**." He holds that such information can only be the product of an intelligent agent. This is a contemporary echo of the **natural theology** argument that was articulated by William Paley (1743–1805) at the beginning of the 19th century. Paley had famously proposed that, just as a watch found on a heath is evidence of a human designer, so a complex phenomenon found in nature (such as the human eye) is evidence of a supernatural designer.

The second claim of "intelligent design," first presented by Behe, is that some biological structures and processes are **irreducibly complex**. The bacterial flagellum has often been cited as a case in point. This is the motor-like extension to a bacterium cell that allows it to propel itself. Another frequently cited example is the blood clotting cascade, which is a series of chemical reactions that occur to stop the flow of blood from a wound.

According to Behe, it is highly unlikely that all the necessary parts of such complex systems could have been acquired sequentially through small incremental changes by means of the evolutionary mechanisms of random mutations and natural selection. He has claimed that none of the parts by themselves have a function, so there would be no selective advantage in their acquisition. Behe argues that it would be virtually impossible for the necessary parts — even if they had evolved simultaneously — to suddenly come together in an integrated way to operate effectively. The only explanation available, he claims, is that such phenomena must be caused by an Intelligent Designer.

While proposing these arguments as alternatives to natural evolutionary explanations, neither Dembski nor Behe have offered any detailed account of natural history in light of their proposals. They have, however, suggested general scenarios for how this Intelligence might work. One possibility is that the Designer could intervene at critical points in history to inject new information into natural systems from outside of nature. A second possibility is that the Designer could have imbued ultimate designs into the first cells of life. In other words, "irreducibly complex" biochemical structures could lie dormant as potentials in cells until they are called forth.

"Intelligent design" advocates are usually careful not to identify the Designer when presenting their views in academic or political settings. Some of the proponents have even suggested that the Designer could be an extraterrestrial. However, this possibility only raises the question of who or what designed that Designer and so leads to an infinite regression of designers or an ultimate undesigned Designer. However, when talking with religious communities, ID promoters are often explicit in affirming their view that the "Intelligent Designer" is God.

Some ID proponents have argued that science must be modified at its foundations in order to allow supernatural causes to be included in scientific theories. This would mean abandoning the longstanding and fundamental principle that limits scientific explanations to natural causes. Phillip Johnson, who has urged such a modification, calls this proposed form of inquiry "theistic science."

Well-educated Christians have been attracted to "intelligent design" for several reasons. Some of its proponents are scientists from major universities and not just advocates from small fringe creationist organizations. The scientific credentials of these advocates give their position more apparent credibility before the nonscientific public. "Intelligent design" does not require that one accept either biblical literalism or the doctrine of a young Earth and a six-day creation. In fact, it does not even require one to deny evolution altogether.

For example, "intelligent design" does not rule out the possibility that natural selection acts upon variety within a species so that bacteria could evolve antibiotic resistance. Such evolutionary change is often called **microevolution**. It is the evolution of new species, a phenomenon of **macroevolution**, that ID proponents challenge. (For evolutionary biologists, micro- and macroevolution are equivalent, differing only with

For some advocates, "intelligent design" does not rule out the possibility that natural selection acts upon variety within a species so that bacteria could evolve antibiotic resistance.

regard to timescale and accompanying degree of biological modification.) The final and most important reason that "intelligent design" has built up a big following is that it is presented as a "theistic scientific" alternative to a strictly naturalistic science, that is, a "science" that identifies God as a clear and identifiable cause of natural events. This appeals to Christians who are favorable toward science and do not want to abandon it.

In recent years, substantial funding from some Christians has supported the political lobbying efforts on behalf of "intelligent design." Among the major backers of ID is the Discovery Institute in the state of Washington, a public policy think tank that also supports free market and libertarian political views. Although fundamentalist advocacy for "scientific" creationism has not disappeared, many of its advocates have joined the ID movement as a potentially effective tool to dislodge evolutionary biology from its place in the science curriculum of the public schools.

A common strategy of ID advocates has been to urge "teaching the controversy" despite the fact that there is no scientific controversy about a natural evolutionary explanation for the diversity of life.

Rather than calling for the outright elimination of evolution from the curriculum, ID advocates commonly seek to reduce or marginalize evolutionary biology by urging that the schools "teach the controversy." By this expression, they imply that there is a real scientific controversy, which there is not. While there are lively debates among evolutionary scientists about particular aspects of the evolutionary process, there is no ongoing scientific dispute about the basic evolutionary claim, namely, that all contemporary forms of life are the result of "descent with modification" (Darwin's term)

Evolution Dialogues

from a common ancestor over the past nearly 4 billion years. The controversy that does exist is not a scientific one but a political and cultural one, promoted by the anti-evolutionists themselves through their campaign for "intelligent design."

The declaration that "evolution is a theory, not a fact" is especially prominent among ID advocates from the most conservative Christian communities. This slogan plays upon common usage of the word "theory" to mean "hunch" or "educated guess." It reflects a misunderstanding of the nature of science. Within science, a theory is the best explanation that is possible for a set of **facts**, which are observations from nature or data from laboratory experiments. Theory building often begins with a curiosity in nature — a puzzling natural phenomenon. A possible explanation, or **hypothesis**, is proposed. On the basis of the hypothesis, additional facts are predicted. If the hypothesis stands up well in the light of such new facts, then the hypothesis will be combined with other well-supported hypotheses into a **theory**, which is an explanation of a natural phenomenon well supported by a wide range of evidence from nature. In other words, a theory is not less than the facts it is built upon. A strong theory is the highest order of knowledge available in science and is the nearest account that science can provide of the truth about nature.

The promotion of "intelligent design" also is often coupled with calls to teach "the evidence against evolution." At present, there is not any such evidence. In fact, the evidence continues to mount supporting the scientific conclusion that evolution has and continues to occur. Generally, when "evidence against evolution" is proposed by ID advocates it is either not relevant to the question on whether evolution occurs, is only relevant to a particular understanding of how it occurs, or is judged by the relevant scientists to be a misunderstanding of the so-called "evidence" itself.

Ultimately, however, the debate over "intelligent design" is not so much about particular observations or scientific findings. Rather, it is about the very nature of the scientific enterprise and whether thorough explanations of the history of nature can be made in terms of nature itself without reference to God. One reason that modern science has flourished since the 17th century, providing ever-deeper understanding of the structures, processes, and history of nature, is that it has limited itself to natural explanations alone. This limitation does not preclude other explanations, in particular, religious explanations or the affirmation of God as the ultimate source of nature. Scientific investigation cannot be satisfied by reference to the mystery of God, but neither does it eliminate that ultimate mystery.

Scientists respond

Although the "intelligent design" hypothesis has been around for two decades, it has produced no credible scientific research to support it. A great deal more money and personal effort has been devoted to lobbying for ID's inclusion in the classroom than has been committed to investigating its scientific validity. A number of popular-press books have been published promoting "intelligent design" to the public. Virtually no original research articles about "intelligent design" have been published in peer-reviewed scientific journals. No such research has been presented at relevant scientific meetings.

On the other hand, a growing number of scientists have examined the claims for "intelligent design" and have found them wanting. Among the most prominent is Kenneth R. Miller (1948–), professor of cell biology at Brown University. He has lectured, testified, debated, and written in defense of the scientific integrity of evolutionary theory and in rebuttal of the claim that "intelligent design" has scientific credibility. A practicing Roman Catholic, Miller published a book in 1999 entitled *Finding Darwin's God: A Scientist's Search for Common Ground Between God and Evolution.*

Frank Sonleitner, emeritus professor of zoology at the University of Oklahoma, is another scientist who has challenged the "intelligent design" movement. In 1994, Sonleitner developed a point-by-point scientific critique of the text *Of Pandas and People* that he titled "What's Wrong with Pandas?"

Eugenie Scott (1945–) is another scientist who has been prominent in the challenge to "intelligent design." Scott is an anthropologist and the director of the National Center for Science Education, a nonprofit organization formed in 1981 to support the integrity of science education in the public schools, particularly related to the teaching of evolution. She also is past president of the American Association of Physical Anthropologists. Her 2004 book, *Evolution vs. Creationism,* provides an introduction to the many facets of the current debate over "intelligent design," including the scientific evidence for evolution, the legal and educational basis for its teaching, and the various religious points of view on evolution. There are many other scientists like Miller, Sonleitner, and Scott.

The scientific arguments against "intelligent design" are extensive and some of them are quite complicated. One main point is that the formation of so-called "irreducibly complex" systems can, with sufficiently thorough scientific investigation, be explained through natural causes. To scientists, the fact that a complex phenomenon *has not* yet been explained through natural causes is not evidence for the intervention of an Intelligent Designer. One classic example can illustrate the general thrust of this argument. Kenneth Miller has provided the following description of how a few light-sensitive cells could evolve into the complex eye:

> *Starting with the simplest light-sensing device, a single photoreceptor cell, it is possible to draw a series of incremental changes that would lead directly to the lens-and-retina eye. None of the intermediate stages are unreasonable, since each requires nothing more than an incremental change in structure: an increase in cell number, a change in surface curvature, a slight increase in transparency .... As the saying goes, in the land of the blind the one-eyed man is king. Likewise, in a population with limited ability to sense light, every improvement in vision, no matter how slight, would be favored — and favored dramatically — by natural selection.*[29]

Many species alive today have simple eyes. There are the pit eyes of flatworms, the proto-compound eyes of certain clams, the single-chambered proto-eyes of the Nautilus, and the pinhole eyes of the giant clam, to name a few.

© Courtesy of: Jan Messersmith

Flatworms, crocodiles, and mammals represent diverse results in the evolution of eyes.

These eye types represent transitional stages involved in the evolution of the lens-and-retina eye. At the same time, by their persistence in today's natural world, they represent real, adaptive solutions for particular organisms in their particular environments. Likewise, using examples from the natural world as well as laboratory observations, scientists have explained how the individual parts that form the complex features of organisms (such as the bacterium flagellum and the blood clotting cascade) could have independently evolved with other functions. Over time, step by step through natural selection, those parts adaptively combined to form the more complex systems with newly emergent functions. Thus, such complex systems cannot accurately be described as "irreducibly complex."

A keystone arch is irreducibly complex but can be formed step by step by first erecting a scaffold that is removed when the arch is complete. "Scaffolding" is also employed in nature to increase complexity.

Another scientific challenge to the idea of "irreducible complexity" invokes the metaphor of the keystone arch. Such an arch cannot stand without its center stone. In that way, it is "irreducibly complex." However, when an arch is constructed, the builders use scaffolding to hold up the structure until the keystone is inserted. Then they remove the scaffolding. In like manner, certain components of living systems appear to have been dropped into place as if by magic or miracle. Yet they too can be explained by the existence of prerequisite parts that later disappeared through the evolutionary process once the primary structure was formed.

In this regard, scientists point out that living organisms have many extra, apparently useless parts: repeated or unused strands of code in the DNA, atrophied leg bones in whales, and the human appendix, to name three examples. Findings through comparative biology suggest that these parts had functions in ancestral populations and in some cases may have served as "scaffolding" but have atrophied and are now being discarded over generations as part of the evolutionary development of the organism. "intelligent design" cannot explain the existence of these vestigial parts.

Another important point scientists make is that complex phenomena in nature are flawed and hardly seem the product of intelligent forethought. The eye is a case in point. The eye's optic nerve connecting cells in the eye to the brain cuts right through the back of the retina, creating a blind spot. In contrast, the mollusk eye is differently organized, with nerve cells beneath the light-sensitive cells rather than in front of them. The mollusk eye has no blind spot, though it has its own imperfections.

By studying embryos in development, scientists have learned that the human eye emerges outward from brain cells, while the mollusk eye develops inward from skin cells. This accounts for the different layering of nerve cells and light-sensitive cells. Evolutionary theory explains how eye structure emerges through the accumulation of small changes. Each adaptive change enhanced survival in some small way but did necessarily produce the most efficient or elegant overall design. "Intelligent design" offers no coherent explanation for such imperfections.

Evolution Dialogues

"Intelligent design" presumes that the actions of a supernatural Intelligent Designer can be detected through scientific inquiry. But supernatural entities by definition operate outside of natural laws and so cannot be investigated using the methods of observation and experimentation. Thus, "intelligent design" encourages the abandonment of scientific inquiry about natural causes by prematurely asserting an ultimate cause. In 2001, the Public Broadcasting System produced a documentary series about evolution. Its companion book, named *Evolution: The Triumph of an Idea,* explains the problem:

> *When microbiologists study an outbreak of resistant tuberculosis, they do not research the possibility that it is an act of God. When astrophysicists try to figure out the sequence of events by which a primordial cloud condensed into our solar system, they do not simply draw a big box between the hazy cloud and the well-formed planets and write inside it, "Here a miracle happened." When meteorologists fail to predict the path of a hurricane, they do not claim that God's will pushed it off course. Science cannot simply cede the unknown in nature to the divine.*[30]

Human eyes have a "blind spot" because the optic nerve passes through the back of the retina. In contrast, in the eyes of mollusks, the nerve cells lie below the light-sensing cells, requiring no break in them. In this regard, the mollusk's eye is functionally better than the human eye.

Science is replete with examples of previously mysterious mechanisms that are now at least partially understood: what causes fire (explained by combustion theory), what causes disease (elucidated by germ theory), what causes tornados (explicated through meteorological theory), etc. It is the "unknown in nature" that is grist for the scientific mill, stimulus for the scientific imagination, and spur for scientific inquiry into the deeper depths of nature.

As with "creation science" before it, "intelligent design" has been tested in the federal courts. In 2005, a suit was entered by parents in Dover, PA, against the local school board for instituting a policy encouraging the study of "intelligent design" in biology classes. The judgment of the court was that the school board policy was a violation of the establishment clause of the First Amendment of the U.S. Constitution. In addition, the federal judge ruled that "intelligent design" is not science, but rather "an interesting theological argument."

Paleontologist
Stephen Jay Gould.

Creation and evolution as complementary

The public controversy over evolution has been fractious and noisy. As such, it has often obscured the range of contemporary Christian responses to evolution. As described earlier, one response has been to begin with particular religious commitments and to transform or distort science to make it conform to those commitments. From this perspective, standard science is viewed as a threat to traditional Christianity and so it is challenged. Individual Christians from a range of denominations fall into this category and it is they who today energize the "intelligent design" movement.

However, many Christians have no more grievances with the science of evolution than they do with other scientific theories such as those found in astronomy or quantum physics. This is because they hold the idea that science and religion constitute "different, but complementary, forms of truth," a view that has been characterized by the phrase "nonoverlapping magisteria." Magisteria means teaching authorities. The expression was coined by paleontologist Stephen Jay Gould in a 1997 article he wrote for *Natural History Magazine.* Gould argued that science and religion are two ways of knowing that do not conflict because of the "lack of overlap between their respective domains of professional expertise — science in the empirical constitution of the universe, and religion in the search for proper ethical values and the spiritual meaning of our lives."

This is not a new view. It developed in the aftermath of the controversy between Galileo and the church. It is the view represented in the works of perhaps the most influential Protestant theologian of the 20th century, Karl Barth. For Barth, science and theology ought not intersect because each has its own distinctive methods and objects of study.

For the vast majority of Roman Catholics, Bible interpretation has never been limited to the literal sense of the text. The Catholic Church had no objection to scientific evidence for an evolving universe. Church teaching holds that evolutionary theory is "more than a hypothesis," in the words of the late Pope John Paul II (1920–2005), who wrote that "this theory has been progressively accepted by researchers, following a series of discoveries in various fields of knowledge. The convergence, neither sought nor fabricated, of the results of work that was conducted independently is in itself a significant argument in favor of this theory." One caveat to evolution noted by John Paul was the Catholic teaching that God directly delivered ("infused") the soul into the first and subsequent human beings, and it is this union of body and soul that constitutes the truly human person and distinguishes humanity from the rest of creation.

The **mainline churches** have not found evolution in conflict with their teachings. These are Protestant denominations with moderate theologies that attempt to be open to new ideas and societal changes without abandoning what they consider to be the historical basis of the Christian faith. Many of these denominations have taken formal positions in support of teaching the scientific theory and against what they consider to be the imposition of religious doctrine ("scientific" creationism or "intelligent design") on public school science education. These include the Lutheran World Federation, the Episcopal Church USA, the Presbyterian Church (USA), the United Church of Christ, and the United Methodist Church.

In recent years, Christians have been taking more public stances in support of evolutionary theory, for a variety of reasons. One reason is to affirm that Christianity has historically encouraged scientific inquiry. Another reason is to show that faith in God as Creator can be consistent with an evolutionary understanding of the history of the universe and particularly life on Earth. But for some perhaps the most important reason is that evolutionary theory stimulates in positive ways their own evolving understanding of God.

In 2005 the Episcopal Church published a lengthy "Catechism of Creation" that includes an evolutionary understanding of the history of life.

As a recent example, the Presbyterian Church (USA) adopted a resolution in 2002 reaffirming that "there is no contradiction between an evolutionary theory of human origins and the doctrine of God as Creator." The resolution encouraged state boards of education to establish standards for science education in public schools based on the recommendations of the scientific community, and it called upon Presbyterian scientists and science educators to work toward greater public understanding of what constitutes reliable scientific knowledge.

Even more recently, in 2005, the Episcopal Church published a lengthy "Catechism of Creation" that explains in question-and-answer format how the Bible's doctrine of creation can be understood as consistent with an evolutionary scientific worldview. "The Bible, including Genesis, is not a divinely dictated scientific textbook," it says in part. "We discover scientific knowledge about God's universe in nature not Scripture."

These institutional positions have been matched by individual demonstrations of support for evolution. As just one example of this trend, more than 10,000 clergy across the country have signed a statement that was first circulated in 2004 to protest anti-evolution policies passed by the local school board in Grantsburg, Wisconsin. It reads in part: "We the undersigned, Christian clergy from many different traditions, believe that the timeless truths of the Bible and the discoveries of modern science may comfortably coexist .... We ask that science remain science and that religion remain religion, two very different, but complementary, forms of truth." This statement suggests a two-realms view of the science and religion relationship similar to Gould's "nonoverlapping magisteria," a view in which science and religion stand as separate but equal domains.

Creation and evolution as interactive

There are questions that cannot be addressed if science and religion are kept separate. How exactly would God operate through the details of evolution? If biological evolution is directionless and contingent, what does it say about divine purpose? If there is divine purpose, can it be discerned? If human beings are subject to extinction or to evolutionary transformation, what does it mean to say they are made in the image of God? Such questions have stimulated the search for constructive engagement between science and the Christian faith.

Many people have contributed to this burgeoning field of scholarship, but among the most important has been Ian Barbour (1923–). A physicist who also has a graduate degree in theology, Barbour published *Issues in Science and Religion* in 1966. In this landmark work, Barbour offered a typology for the ways in which science and religion can relate. As he saw it, these ways include not only conflict and independence but also dialogue and integration. He illustrated this typology with a great many specific references to earlier theological scholarship.

One of the most provocative theologians that Barbour cited was the French Jesuit paleontologist, Pierre Teilhard de Chardin (1881–1955) [*The Human Phenomenon,* 1959/1999]. As a paleontologist, Teilhard was part of the French research team that discovered Peking Man, a fossil specimen belonging to the hominin species *Homo erectus.* Teilhard was intrigued by the inherent dynamism in the evolutionary processes of nature and wondered how that same dynamism might reflect divine activity in creation. Teilhard's rethinking of Christian theology in the light of evolution viewed God as continuously and intimately engaged in an ongoing creation of the universe through the evolutionary processes.

Because Teilhard's approach was toward an integration of science and theology, his work was viewed with skepticism by both his scientific and religious communities. In fact, most of his theological writings were published after his death in 1955, because he was prohibited by his religious community from teaching or publishing his views. Teilhard's theology is sometimes called **evolutionary theology** because of its effort to integrate an evolutionary scientific understanding of nature with a Christian theology of creation. The late Karl Schmitz-Moormann (1928–1996) [*Theology of Creation in an Evolutionary World*, 1997] carried forward Teilhard's effort with the conviction that "[t]heology now must adopt a new view, in which this evolving universe is perceived as the continued self-revelation of the Creator."

Contemporary theologians are also exploring the interaction of science and religion. Two British scientists turned Anglican theologians illustrate two leanings among those who see an opportunity for constructive interaction between the evolutionary sciences and traditional Christian theology. John Polkinghorne (1930–) [*The Faith of a Physicist*, 1996], physicist-turned-theologian, views the sciences as informing and enriching theological reflection on traditional questions like the meaning of God as Creator and God's ongoing relationship with the creation. In contrast, Arthur Peacocke (1924–) [*Creation and the World of Science*, 2004], a chemist-turned-theologian, sees in contemporary science and especially evolutionary biology a stimulus for transforming traditional Christian theological affirmations.

Lutheran Philip Hefner [*The Human Factor*, 1993] has drawn upon evolutionary biology as well as cultural anthropology to reconsider a Christian understanding of human nature in an evolving universe. He has identified humans as created co-creators of the world with God. Wentzel van Huyssteen [*Alone in the World?*, 2006], a Reformed theologian, constructively draws upon contemporary scientific studies of human evolution, **paleoanthropology**, to express a Christian theological understanding of human nature as an emergent phenomenon of the evolution of **hominins**.

Some Christian religious scholars suggest that God creates the world by enabling it to create itself and that God is affected by the evolution of the universe. This position is called **process theology**, and among its adherents are John Cobb [*A Christian Natural Theology*, 1965], a Methodist theologian, and John Haught, a theologian in the Roman Catholic tradition. In the words of Haught [*God After Darwin*, 2001], God is the source "of order but also of novelty," and "it is the introduction of novelty into the world that makes evolution possible."

Christians today exhibit a wide range of approaches in relation to science. For Christians who see contemporary science as a threat to cherished religious beliefs, the tendency is either to discredit or to distort science. Other Christians find satisfaction by placing at least elements of evolutionary science and theologies of creation in separate compartments of knowledge. Still other Christians have chosen the task of developing a Christian theology of creation that is coherent with an evolutionary understanding of nature. How does Christian theology relate to the sciences of evolution? What is demonstrably clear is that there is no one answer to this question.

FURTHER READING

The Creationists, Ronald L. Numbers (University of California Press, 1993)

Can a Darwinian be a Christian? Michael Ruse (Cambridge University Press, 2001)

Evolution vs. Creationism: An introduction, Eugenie C. Scott (Greenwood Press, 2004)

Finding Darwin's God: A scientist's search for common ground between God and evolution, Kenneth R. Miller (Harper Perennial, 2000)

God and Nature: Historical essays on the encounter between Christianity and science, David C. Lindberg and Ronald L. Numbers, ed. (University of California Press, 1986)

Responses to 101 Questions on God and Evolution, John F. Haught (Paulist Press, 2001)

Rocks of Ages: Science and Religion in the Fullness of Life, Stephen Jay Gould (Ballantine Books, 2002)

When Science and Christianity Meet, David C. Lindberg and Ronald L. Numbers, eds. (University of California Press, 2003)

Advancing beyond dialogue

The auditorium was emptying out after the evening's program on "The Evolution of Life Elsewhere." Angela Rawlett walked up the center aisle, closely followed by a young man holding a laptop and with headphones draped around his neck. As she approached the last row of seats, she noticed a man gathering up papers into a briefcase. It was Phil Compton, the minister who had served as her religious advisor over the past year.

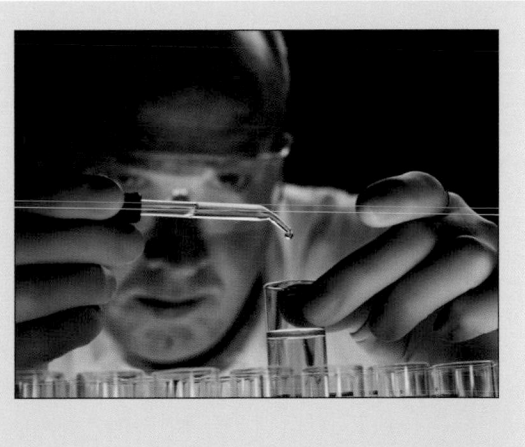

"So you came!" said Angela by way of greeting.

Phil stood up. "I'm glad I did." He reached over to shake her hand, and Angela realized it was the first time she had ever seen him when he wasn't drinking coffee.

"And your friend is?" Phil asked.

"Oh," said Angela, turning around as though noticing the young man for the first time. "This is Lenny Baillard. A friend of mine. My lab partner. Lenny, this is Phil Compton. He works in Campus Ministry."

Lenny gave a vague wave in Phil's direction. "That's it," he said excitedly to Angela. "That's it. I'm changing my major to chemistry."

Phil looked mystified.

"Those experiments they talked about tonight, turning chemicals into amino acids. *It's alive!*"

"Frankenstein, I believe," said Phil. "But as they explained tonight, creating life in the lab wouldn't be quite like that."

"Yeah, I know," the student responded. "But still, synthesizing life. What a rush." He turned to Angela. "You Jane, me God!"

Angela looked both amused and annoyed by Lenny's remarks. "You idiot," she grinned at him. Turning to Phil, she added, "It is pretty wild. It hadn't ever occurred to me before that the first aliens we ever meet might come from a test tube and not from Mars."

Bounding up the aisle two steps at a time, Dr. Laurel Dunbar joined the cluster. "Wasn't that *fascinating*? Who cares about alien creatures? I care about plants. At least one of those other planets out there must have something like an orchid."

Angela introduced the biology professor to her religious advisor and was a little startled to learn that the two knew each other.

"And this is Lenny Baillard," Angela said. "Lenny thinks that if he creates life in the lab, that makes him God. What do you think?"

Dr. Dunbar stared intently into Lenny's face. "So this is what God would look like?"

"Really," said Angela. "What do you think?"

"Speaking as a scientist, Angela, I can neither define God nor identify God at work."

"Then don't speak as a scientist," says Angela. "Speak as a person, and tell me what you really think."

"Alright," said Dr. Dunbar, rubbing her chin slightly. "Speaking as just a person, then — I would say that no, synthesizing life would not make Mr. Baillard God."

Angela grinned broadly, and it was Lenny's turn to look annoyed. "Why not?" he asked the professor.

"Test tube experiments are feeble compared to what it takes to create the diversity of the living world," Dr. Dunbar responded, with some passion. "Besides, who puts the beakers in your hands? Who gives you the chemicals and the energy — and the ideas? I'd suggest God does. Lenny, you are not God."

"Given that Lenny is human," interjected Phil, "we have to consider how he would manage his god-like power over his synthesized microbes. What responsibilities would he have toward them?"

"And what if we humans find life on another planet?" Lenny asked back. "Do we go down the same old takeover and colonizing trip that we've been on for the past centuries?"

"Why speculate?" interjected Dr. Dunbar. "Why not ask what we do right now with our god-like powers over other forms of life on Earth, many of which are still as alien and undiscovered as any life that might be galaxies away?"

There was a silent though not disagreeable tension within the group. "Classes end next week," said Phil in a lighter tone. "I haven't asked you what you'll be doing this summer, Angela."

"For the first part I'm going to be a counselor at my church camp like I've done for the past three years. But in August I'm going on that paleo dig in South Dakota organized by Dr. Brown."

"You got into that?" asked Lenny. "I'm wait-listed. How did you get in?"

"What attracts you to the dig?" Phil cut in, before Angela could reply to her fellow student. "I thought you enjoyed working with live animals. Any mammals you dig up there will have been dead for millions of years."

Angela laughed. "I want to experience that awesome sense of time," she responded. "To see a creature lying where it fell so long ago, millions of years before any human walked the earth."

"What does your father think of this plan?" asked Dr. Dunbar.

"He thinks fossils are fascinating, just like I do," said Angela. "I suppose we disagree about where fossils came from, but we'll have time enough to talk about that. He's going to drive me up there and stay a couple days. "

Lenny scowled. "Your *dad* is on the dig and I'm wait-listed?"

Phil followed with another question. "What inspired you to make this choice?"

"*'Join us in the trenches of science!'*" exclaimed Angela. "*"See how knowledge builds from small discoveries!'* Those are Dr. Brown's words."

The White River Badlands in the Badlands National Park in South Dakota contains some of the richest and most diverse Oligocene fossil beds in the world with specimens 34 to 24 million years old.

"There's something romantic about being out there, in the soil and sun," said Dr. Dunbar.

"It'll be hot and sweaty," countered Lenny. "You'll just be a grunt."

"I'll be a grunt in one of the most stunning landscapes on Earth."

"It is mysterious territory," said Phil. "It's one of those places where the presence of God is almost palpable."

"I've heard that," said Angela. "That's one reason I'm so excited. Do you know what I think would be the neatest thing?"

Lenny muttered something about seeing a brontothere rise up from the dead.

Angela heard what he said and smiled at him. "Sure, Lenny, that'd be pretty cool. But I was thinking about a sunrise service, right there at the dig. I'm going to go to one, even if I have to organize it myself."

Advancing beyond dialogue

The immediate issues have been resolved for Angela Rawlett, the protagonist of the story weaving through *The Evolution Dialogues.* She is taking her required biology classes, which address evolution. She is maintaining her Christian faith. She is seeking ways to constructively relate her science with her faith tradition. She continues to be curious and inquiring. She has overcome her anxiety about what she may learn and what she may become.

How will Angela grow as a scientist and a Christian? The answer to that question remains for each reader to imagine. We can all see, however, that several paths are open by which she might continue developing as a scientist *and* faithfully participate in her religious community. What makes these paths possible is that science and the Christian tradition share certain values.

Perhaps the most obvious shared value is *truthfulness.* Drawing from their Hebraic roots, Christians are committed to "not bearing false witness." The practice of science depends fundamentally on recording and reporting data truthfully. Both science and Christianity fail when either shortchanges the truth. Political disputes over the teaching of evolution in the public schools often exhibit an absence of this value. The old adage that one should "emphasize the positive and eliminate the negative" becomes a rationale for being less than fully truthful about what science says, what Christians believe, and who speaks for science or for Christianity, among other things. Both scientists and Christians have common cause in calling for truthfulness in all such matters.

Another shared value is that of *community.* Neither science nor Christianity is a socially isolated reality. In fact, relationship in community is essential for each. Though scientists test their theories against nature, it is other scientists who judge the outcomes of these tests. Though Christians have organized themselves in a variety of social structures, all of them depend in

In the United States, many scientists are active members of Christian communities. They play an important role in determining how evolution and Christianity will relate to one another.

one way or another upon the judgment of the community. Individual conscience is honored, but ultimately assessed within the community of faith — just as any individual scientific insight must pass muster from the collective community of scientists. Scientists and people of faith together participate in the larger community of the United States and increasingly in a global community. The good of that larger community depends in this day to a great deal on how science and religious traditions of the world relate to one another.

Tradition is another shared value. Isaac Newton said that he "stood on the shoulders of giants." By this he recognized that his own accomplishments were dependent upon the insights of those before him who had sought to understand the structure and processes of the world. Contemporary evolutionary theory is significantly different from the way Charles Darwin originally formulated it in 1859, by virtue of the addition of insights from genetics and molecular biology that were not available in his time. But in a traditional sense, contemporary evolutionary theory is Darwinian, in that Darwin's basic insight into the interplay of variation among offspring and selective pressures from the environment still provides the basic framework for an understanding of the history of life. In the same way, contemporary Christian beliefs and forms of religious practice can be traced along lines of tradition stretching back some 2,000 years. It is also the case that the scientific tradition and the Christian tradition have been intertwined over that same period, sometimes in tension, sometimes constructively, but always dynamically.

And one more shared value is that of analytic *reason*. It is the rational deduction of laboratory tests or sought-after empirical observations from hypotheses, and the critical analysis of test and observational data that is the backbone of the scientific method. The Christian tradition is grounded in a text, the Bible, which is neither systematic nor simple in its religious expression. It is through the exercise of analytic reason that systematic bodies of doctrine have been developed and are assessed. Reason is a commonly valued tool that should allow scientists drawing an evolutionary picture of the world and Christians who see that world as a creation to discover opportunities for consonance.

Those scientists and Christians who argue that contemporary evolutionary theory and contemporary Christian theology are inherently at odds, only do so by denying the very values that science and Christianity hold in common. They are being less than truthful, are denying the broader community in which both are dependent, are ignoring the historical interaction of scientific and Christian traditions, and are so selective in their use of reason as to distort its results.

In the United States, many scientists are Christians, though relatively few Christians (or Americans for that matter) are scientists. Yet everyone, Christian and non-Christian alike, benefits from the fruits of science, for example, from better understandings of energy, medicine, and ecological dynamics. We will lose these benefits if science education is undermined either by those who claim that science is the source of all answers or by those who claim that scientific answers are only legitimate if they conform to a narrow set of Christian doctrines that ignore much of what is understood about the natural world.

Scientists who also stand in the Christian community — like the scientist Angela hopes to become — have the unique opportunity to embody the common cause. They can show fellow Christians how science adds to religious understanding, so that, for example, as science reveals the workings of nature, one can better discern how "the heavens declare" and "the Earth shows forth" the glory of God's handiwork. They can be exemplars of a Christian ethical tradition that enables them to work with discipline and integrity, frame interesting scientific questions, review evidence objectively, obtain useful insights, interpret results without hubris, and consider the broader impact of the work in the lives of other people. Finally, they can model the humility that religious believers ought to have when interpreting science and scientists ought to have when interpreting religion.

CHAPTER 1

1. Jack Repcheck, *The Man Who Found Time: James Hutton and the Earth's antiquity.* Perseus Publishing, 2003, p. 17.

CHAPTER 2

2. The biblical quotes in this chapter are taken from the King James translation, which was the most common Protestant version of the Bible in use in the 19th century.

3. *The Literal Meaning of Genesis (De Genesi ad litteram libri duodecim)* (translated by J. H. Taylor, Ancient Christian Writers, Newman Press, 1982, volume 41), Book 1, Chapter 19, Paragraph 39.

4. Francis Bacon, in *The Advancement of Learning*, First Book, I, 3.

5. Galileo Galilei: Letter to the Grand Duchess Christina of Tuscany, 1615, quoted in Modern History Sourcebook, http://www.fordham.edu/halsall/mod/galileo-tuscany.html.

6. Edward J. Larson, *Evolution: The remarkable history of a scientific theory.* Modern Library, 2004, pp. 34–35.

7. F. Darwin, ed., *The Life and Letters of Charles Darwin*, vol. II, London, 1887, p. 218.

8. F. Darwin, ed., *op. cit.*, vol. I, pp. 315–316.

9. F. Darwin, ed., *op. cit.*, vol. II, p. 312.

10. Charles Darwin from a manuscript in the Darwin archive of the Cambridge University Library, quoted in Randal Keynes, *Darwin, His Daughter & Human Evolution.* Riverhead Books, 2002, pp. 351–352.

11. F. Darwin, ed., *op. cit.*, vol. I, p. 304.

CHAPTER 4

12. Janet Browne, *Charles Darwin*, New York, Alfred A. Knopf, 2002, vol. 2, p. 87.

13. Adam Sedgwick, from a letter to Charles Darwin on November 24, 1859, cited at the University of California – Berkeley Museum of Paleontology website: http://www.ucmp.berkeley.edu/history/sedgwick.html.

14. Brian W. Harrison, "Early Vatican responses to evolutionist theology," in *Living Tradition: Organ of the Roman Theological Forum*. No. 93, May 2001, p. 1, http://www.rtforum.org/lt/lt93.html.

15. Thomas Henry Huxley, "The Reception of 'The Origin of Species,'" in F. Darwin, ed., *op. cit.*, vol. II, p. 196.

16. J. Browne, *op. cit.*, p. 93.

17. J. Browne, *op. cit.*, p. 95.

18. Baden Powell, "On the study of the evidences of Christianity," in *Essays and Reviews*, London, Longman, Green, Longman, and Roberts, 1860, p. 139.

───

CHAPTER 5

19. Charles Darwin, *On the Origin of Species by Means of Natural Selection, or the preservation of favoured races in the struggle for life*, 6th edition, 1872, p. 177.

20. Charles Darwin, *op. cit.*, p. 54.

21. *Ibid.*

───

CHAPTER 6

22. The names James and Jesus are English versions of Greek translations of Aramaic names with Hebrew roots; Jacob and Joshua, respectively.

23. John Haught, *God after Darwin*, Westview Press, 1999, p. 27.

24. Huston Smith, *Why Religion Matters: The fate of the human spirit in an age of disbelief*. HarperCollins Publishers, Inc., 2001, p. 3.

───

CHAPTER 7

25. James Shreeve, "Craig Venter's epic voyage to redefine the origin of the species," in *Wired Magazine*, August 2004, p. 1.

26. There is a caveat to this claim about all living organisms having DNA. A virus is a very simple organism that only can reproduce by hitchhiking inside the cell of another organism as it divides. Some viruses only have RNA (which helps DNA build proteins) and borrow the DNA of their hosts. Because they cannot carry on life's functions independently, scientists do not consider viruses to be living in the way that other organisms are. But viruses have had a big impact on the course of evolution, because as they move between species, they cart DNA back and forth and thereby introduce genetic changes into species.

27. Janet Larsen, "The Sixth Great Extinction: a status report," Earth Policy Institute, Update 35: March 2, 2004.

───

CHAPTER 8

28. Jill Burcum, "Kid's book on evolution stirs censorship debate in Monticello," *Minnesota Star Tribune*, May 12, 2005.

29. Kenneth R. Miller, "Life's grand design," *Technology Review*, February/March 1994, Volume 97 (2): 24–32.

30. Carl Zimmer, *Evolution: The triumph of an idea*. HarperCollins Publishers, Inc., 2001, p. 333.

adaptive. A term used to describe genotypes or phenotypes that are beneficial within a given environment such that they improve an organism's ability to survive and reproduce.

agnostic. One who neither believes nor disbelieves in God and holds that the question of God's existence is unanswerable.

allele. One of two or more variants of a given gene. For example, one allele of a gene for human eye color codes for blue eyes, while another codes for brown eyes.

amphibians. Animals that are aquatic and breathe through gills as juveniles and are terrestrial and breathe through lungs as adults.

analogies. Similar characteristics that develop in widely separated species generally because of adaptive pressure in similar ecological contexts.

archaea. Single-celled organisms genetically distinct from bacteria that tend to live in extreme environments such as superhot or supercold water.

archetypes. A term used by Richard Owen, a contemporary and critic of Darwin, to describe the basic structural plans that he believed were adapted by God to form each different species in the creation process.

argument from design. The position that evidence of order in the universe (such as the discovery of natural laws and complex structure of organs and organisms) is evidence for the existence of God.

arthropods. Animals with an outside skeleton or exoskeleton, segmented body, jointed legs, and bilateral symmetry (mirror image right and left sides).

astrobiology. The branch of science that addresses the question of whether there is life on other planets.

atheist. One who believes that God does not exist.

axiom. A statement accepted as true as the basis for argument or inference.

bacteria. Single-celled organisms without a nucleus that constitute, along with archaea and eukarya, one of the three most basic branches of life.

Bible. A set of texts written by a variety of authors over a long period and formally assembled in the first centuries of the Christian community into one collection. The Bible includes works from the sacred texts of Judaism (referred to as the Old Testament), and a set of books that contain accounts of Jesus's life (the Gospels), a history of the early Christian communities, discussions about the nature of God and other religious questions, and personal correspondence (together called the New Testament).

biblical inerrancy. The view that the Bible is without error in every detail.

biblical infallibility. The belief that the Bible makes no mistakes in regard to what it teaches so that when the plain or literal reading of some portions of the Bible are contradictory to reason or experience, they can be read as metaphor, allegory, or parable. This view holds that the Bible is not intended to teach science.

Big Bang theory. The theory, supported by a wide range of evidence, that the universe originated approximately 13.7 billion years ago when an infinitesimally small and unimaginably hot region expanded explosively.

biogeographers. Those who study the distribution and dispersal of species.

Cambrian explosion. A period spanning approximately 30 million years during which a great variety of marine life appeared, created new habitats, and exhibited new behaviors such as burrowing and active hunting. Most of the major body plans (phyla) of modern animals are first preserved in the fossil record from this era, along with many unusual phyla unlike anything alive today.

cells. The microscopic structural units that comprise the physical bodies of all living things.

chloroplasts. Structures within plant cells that turn light energy from the sun into chemical energy to power the plant.

Christ. A title for Jesus meaning "anointed one;" it is the Greek translation of the Hebrew word for Messiah.

Christianity. The traditional system of beliefs and practices centered on the affirmation of Jesus of Nazareth as Son of God and savior from sin.

co-evolution. Evolutionary change that results from interactions between species and between adjacent populations of the same species.

complex specified information. An expression used by "intelligent design" proponents used to characterize features of the natural world that they believe must be the work of an intelligent agent.

convergent evolution. The process that results in similar characteristics that develop in widely separated species generally because of adaptive pressure in similar ecological contexts.

creationism. The belief that God creates the universe. Although the term can refer to a wide range of views, it is commonly used to refer to the belief that the creation took place in six 24-hour days and that each creature, including and especially humans, was created as a distinct kind.

creed. A formal statement of religious belief.

crustaceans. The set of organisms that includes shrimp, crab, lobster, and barnacles.

cultural evolution. The structural change of a society and its values over time.

DNA. Deoxyribonucleic acid. A molecule consisting of two long chains of nucleotides twisted into a double helix and joined by hydrogen bonds between the complementary bases. DNA carries genetic instructions for the biological development of all cellular forms of life and many viruses. DNA is inherited and used to propagate traits. During reproduction, it is replicated and transmitted to off-spring.

DNA sequence. A segment of base pairs along a strand of DNA.

data. Recorded observations or experimental measurements used to develop or evaluate an hypothesis.

day-age theory. An interpretation of the first chapter of Genesis in which each day of creation symbolizes an entire epoch.

denominations. Divisions of the major Christian groups (Roman Catholic, Protestant, etc.) that include Anglicans, Baptists, Presbyterians, Methodists, and hundreds of others.

doctrines. A set of teachings or beliefs on a particular topic, e.g, the doctrine of creation.

empirical evidence. Direct observations from nature as contrasted with intuitive knowledge or speculation.

empirical inquiry. Inquiry based on sensory experience or observation.

endosymbiosis. The formation of mutually dependent relationships by single-celled organisms that results in a major evolutionary innovation; e.g., the emergence of the eukarya (single-celled organisms with nuclei) from prokariotic bacteria.

enlightenment. In Eastern religions, a blessed state in which an individual transcends desire and suffering.

eugenics. A social philosophy based on the idea that some humans are biologically more advanced or evolved than others, and concerned with advancing human evolution through either voluntary or politically mandated social policies that affect human reproduction, such as immigration restrictions on persons from some regions or sterilization of the mentally handicapped.

eukaryotes. Organisms in which genetic code is organized into chromosomes and contained in a nucleus.

evangelical Christianity. A form of Christianity that emphasizes personal religious experience and faith, the importance of being "reborn" in Jesus Christ, and proselytizing outreach to "nonbelievers."

evolutionary developmental biology ("Evo devo"). An emerging field focuses on the evolutionary impact of changes that occur in the DNA that turns genes on and off in the process of the development of the organism. Different species may have the same or similar genes but those genes are regulated differently.

evolutionary theology. A reformulation of Christian theology in the light of evolution suggesting that the world was not created at one moment by God, but rather that God is continuously and intimately engaged in its ongoing creation.

experience. The fact or state of having been affected by or gained knowledge through direct observation or participation.

extinction. The disappearance of species from the planet.

fable. A brief tale designed to illustrate a lesson.

facts. In science, observations that have been repeatedly confirmed.

final cause. The end or purpose toward which a thing moves in its development. This is the cause among Aristotle's four classical causes that is related to purpose.

First Cause. Thomas Aquinas' first cosmological proof for the existence of God argues for a First Cause. This proof derives from Aristotle's argument for a Prime Mover.

flood geology. The idea that the existence of fossils and geological formations such as the Grand Canyon can be explained by one recent (within the last 10,000 years) worldwide event, usually identified as the flood of Noah described in the book of Genesis.

fossil. A remnant, impression, or trace of an organism of past geological ages that has been preserved in the Earth's crust.

freethinker. A term used in the early 19th century to described one who believed in God without believing in the authority of organized religion or in the infallibility of the Bible.

fundamentalist Christianity. An offshoot movement of evangelical Christianity that received its name from a series of pamphlets entitled "The Fundamentals: A Testimony to the Truth," which were published between the years 1910 and 1915. The pamphlets reasserted certain ideas that had been called into question by scholars including that the Bible is true and infallible, that Christ was born of a virgin, that Jesus performed miracles, that Jesus died on the cross, and that he came back to life in his own body.

fungi. Plant-like organisms, the most familiar of which are mushrooms, that lack chlorophyll and absorb their nutrients directly from other organisms.

gap theory. An interpretation of the first chapter of Genesis in which there is an immense gap of time between the creation of the heavens and the Earth in the first verse of Genesis and the days of creation in the following verses.

gene. A sequence of DNA that is the basic physical and functional unit of heredity. In general, genes are instructions for producing proteins.

gene pool. The collective assortment of all forms of all genes within a population. A population evolves when its gene pool changes. This change is measured in the frequency of particular versions of genes in the pool over time.

genetic drift. A random statistical effect that occurs only in small, isolated populations in which the gene pool is small enough that chance events can change its makeup substantially. Because of the size of the population, some genes may be lost or their frequencies increase apart from their selective advantage.

genus. A group of closely related species.

God of the Gaps. The religious view that what cannot be currently explained by science (the "gaps" in our knowledge) constitutes evidence of divine or supernatural action.

gospel. The "good news" taught by Jesus of God's love and forgiveness.

great chain of being. An idea first proposed by the ancient Greek philosopher Aristotle as the "Ladder of Nature," suggesting that all things fall into a single, linear order that ascends from basic matter to human beings to God. Each link in the chain represents a distinct form of being, each with its own ideal structure and function.

higher criticism. A scholarly movement in the 18th and 19th centuries that applied critical historical and literary analysis to questions of the authorship and meaning of the books of the Bible. This scholarship often challenged traditional views.

hominin. A taxonomic group including modern humans and all ancestral human species after the split, 5–8 million years ago, with our closest relatives, the chimpanzees.

hominoid. Belonging to the superfamily that includes humans and apes and their unique ancestors. Today, hominid refers to the evolutionary line that led to gorillas and chimps but not humans, and hominin refers to all human species that ever evolved, including extinct ones.

homologies. Structural similarities found across a variety of animal species. For example, the arm of a human, the limb of a dog, and the clawed foot of a bird all share similar arrangements of bones.

hypothesis. A conceptual proposal to explain a set of observations from which additional potential observations are deduced. An hypothesis is tested by seeking these observations either directly from nature or through experiments. An hypothesis can be falsified or strengthened in light of observations but it cannot be "proved."

igneous rock. A type of rock that is made from crystals and formed at very high temperatures from molten material.

inductive reasoning. The building of scientific theories from facts and observations as opposed to deductive reasoning from self-evident truths or first principles. The English philosopher Francis Bacon is considered one of the founders of modern science for his ardent promotion of this form of reasoning.

insect. A class of usually winged arthropod with well-defined body segments and three pairs of legs.

"intelligent design" ("ID"). A social movement that proposes that there is empirical evidence in nature for the existence of an intelligent agent beyond nature.

irreducible complexity. An expression used by "intelligent design" proponent Michael Behe to describe systems that cannot function without all of their parts. Associated with this definition is the assumption that none of the parts can have an independent function. Behe claims that such systems are observable in nature, could not develop through biological evolution, and constitute evidence for the work of an "Intelligent Designer."

isotopic dating. A technique that uses the rate of decay of radioactive elements within rocks and minerals to estimate their age.

Lamarckianism. The pre-Darwinian evolutionary proposal that traits acquired (or diminished) during the lifetime of an organism can be passed on to the offspring.

liturgies. Worship practices.

macroevolution. Trends in evolution that ultimately produce new species of living things. Through various evolutionary agents such as genetic mutation, natural selection, and genetic drift, a population of an existing species acquires enough new characteristics that it is unable to reproduce with members of the originating species.

mainline denominations (mainline churches). The contemporary branches of various older American Protestant denominations from which newer denominations broke off at one time or another in the 19th and 20th centuries. They include the Episcopal Church, the American Baptist Church, the United Methodist Church, the Presbyterian Church (USA), the Evangelical Lutheran Church, and the United Church of Christ.

mammal. A warm-blooded animal that has a backbone, breathes air, produces hair through its skin, bears its young live, and nurses them.

material reductionists. Those who reduce all interpretations of the world to material processes (activities of matter and energy) and deny the existence of any other forms of reality.

Messiah. A Hebrew title for Jesus meaning "anointed one;" translated into Greek as "Christ."

metazoa. Multi-cellular organisms.

methodological naturalism. The principle that science will restrict itself to explanations of nature that make reference only to nature itself.

microbe. A microscopic organism.

microevolution. Genetic change that occurs within a species, for example, bacterial development of antibiotic resistance.

mitochondria. Structures within cells that turn nutrients into energy.

modern synthesis. The mid-20th century integration of genetics into the field of evolutionary biology to create the overarching contemporary theory of evolution.

mutation. Random change to the base-pair sequence in DNA. Mutation is a primary way that variation is introduced into a gene pool.

natural history. A term that emerged in the early 19th century to describe the study and classification of nature.

natural philosophy. A term, in the centuries leading up to the 1800s, for the study of nature.

natural selection. A term describing how the adaptation of organisms to their environment results in different degrees of survival and reproductive success and thereby the differences in their ability to pass on their characteristics to the next generation.

natural theology. The position that the observation of order in the universe (such as the discovery of natural laws or the intricacy of organs) is evidence for the existence of God.

ontological naturalism. The philosophical affirmation that only the natural world exists.

organic succession. An early term for evolution meaning changes in species over time.

paleoanthropology. The study of human evolution primarily through the study of human fossils and early human artifacts.

photosynthesis. The biochemical process in plants by which sunlight is converted to chemical energy.

phylogeny. The evolutionary history or "family tree" of an organism that shows how it is related to other organisms.

phyla. Body plans used to group or classify organisms.

primates. A group of mammals that includes lemurs, monkeys, apes, and humans.

principle of accommodation. The idea that God reveals truth to people as they are able to comprehend it and that as people obtain a greater understanding of the natural world, their sense of the meaning of the Bible can become more subtle and richer.

process theology. A rethinking of Christian theology in light of the philosophy of Alfred North Whitehead, which was significantly informed by the evolutionary sciences.

prokaryotes. Single-celled organisms, including bacteria and archaea, whose genetic material is not contained in a nucleus.

protist. Single-celled organisms such as algae that are neither plants nor animals but have characteristics of both.

punctuated equilibrium. A proposed refinement of evolutionary theory based on the observation from the fossil record that many species are stable for millions of years and then, in a period as brief as a few tens of thousands of years, experience rapid evolutionary change triggered perhaps by major environmental events, such as massive extinction.

RNA. Ribonucleic acid. A molecule similar to DNA that helps in the process of decoding the genetic information carried by DNA in order to produce proteins.

reason. The power of comprehending, inferring, or thinking, especially in orderly ways.

recombination. The process during the formation of the germ cells of an organism whereby there is a shuffling of the parent's genetic code such that the progeny derive a combination of genes different from that of either parent.

religion. An historical tradition of beliefs and practices that conveys an understanding of the meaning of human existence.

revelation. In Christianity, the communication of God to humankind usually identified both with the person of Jesus and with the teachings of the Bible.

rites. Ceremonial practices.

science. A process through which people seek a better understanding of the natural world. Science explains physical phenomena through the formation of theories that are tested and confirmed through empirical observations of nature — what can be seen, heard, tasted, smelled, and touched.

"scientific" creationism. A variation of young Earth creationism that claims to have empirical and scientific support for its theological conviction that the Earth is only 6,000–10,000 years old and that all organisms were created during a period of six 24-hour days as a limited number of distinct kinds.

scientific method. The theory-building process in which observations are made, hypotheses are proposed and tested, and the scientific community, through its professional meetings and journals, judges whether an hypothesis has been sufficiently supported by evidence, and fits together with other tested hypotheses and natural laws, to form a theory.

Scopes Monkey Trial. The popular name given to the 1925 trial of John Scopes, who was prosecuted for violating Tennessee law by teaching evolution in a public school.

sedimentary rock. A type of rock that is formed from particles of older rock, shell, decomposed organisms, and salt that have been compressed together under a body of water.

sexual selection. The theory that competition for mates between individuals of the same sex (typically males) drives the evolution of certain traits that might otherwise be disadvantageous. An example of such a trait favored by sexual selection is the peacock's tail.

Social Darwinism (Social Evolutionism). The idea that some individuals or groups have selective advantages over others because of their innate biological superiority. Proponents of this idea believed that progress would occur if these individuals or groups were allowed to prevail naturally and without interference by government policy or regulation.

special creation. The idea, derived from Genesis, that God created each kind of thing in a unique act.

speciation. The process through which changes over successive generations of organisms cause segments of populations to diverge such that they can no longer breed together.

species. This common biological term has no universally accepted definition but most commonly refers to a group of organisms that naturally interbreeds and produces viable offspring.

strata. Layers of rock in the crust of the Earth. Nicolas Steno, a 17th century priest, was the first to propose that rock layers originally form in a horizontal manner and that, unless disturbed, lower strata are older than higher.

taxonomy. The classification of organisms into related groups.

tetrapods. Any vertebrate that has two pairs of limbs.

theistic evolution. An assimilation of the theory of evolution with the religious affirmation that God is creator, such that evolution is understood as the means by which God has chosen to create.

theology. Rational inquiry into the nature of God or other religious questions; also, the system or school of thought resulting from such inquiry.

theory. A broad explanation of natural structures or processes that is developed from hypotheses that have been strongly supported by evidence produced through rigorous testing. A theory is a comprehensive explanation of how nature works. It is tentative in that it is open, in the like of new observations, to modification or rejection. The goal of science is to form explanatory theories that are well supported by observations.

theory of evolution. The biological theory that all organisms have a common ancestor and that differences between species are due to divergent modifications in successive generations due largely to genetic variation and natural selection. Charles Darwin, who along with Alfred Russel Wallace first described the basic theory, summed it up in three words: descent with modification.

tradition. The customs, beliefs, and cultural artifacts passed from one generation to the next.

transitional fossils. The fossil remains of a creature that exhibits some traits similar to creatures both earlier and later in its line of descent.

transmutation. A term used by 19th century French naturalist Jean-Baptiste Lamarck to describe a process whereby less perfect organisms change into more perfect organisms.

trilobites. Small marine animals that were most abundant some 500 million years ago and in which the prototypical eye may have emerged.

Evolution Dialogues

Trinity. The conception that God is three persons in one substance consisting of the Father, the Son, and the Holy Spirit. This doctrine was adopted initially by the Christian community at the Council of Nicaea in 325 C.E.

uniformitarianism. A theory that common natural processes in operation regularly over great expanses of time create small, steady, and gradual change in the geology of the Earth.

vertebrates. Animals with backbones.

virus. Any of a large group of submicroscopic infectious agents that replicate themselves within the cells of living hosts and often cause disease.

young-Earth creationism. The form of creationism that asserts that the Earth is no more than 10,000 years old and that fossils and geological formations such as the Grand Canyon can be explained by one great worldwide event, usually identified as the flood of Noah described in the book of Genesis.

Deep evolutionary time

A politician once said, "A million dollars here, a million dollars there and pretty soon you are talking about real money." But actually, large numbers are not all that easy to grasp. So, sometimes it is useful to relate large numbers to things that are more close to people's experience. Evolutionary time is sometimes called "deep time" because the numbers are so large. The following three examples provide ways of relating particular milestones in evolutionary history to measures on a 100-foot rope, a set of volumes, or a 24-hour day.

100-foot rope

Big Bang (13,700*) .... 0' 0" the start of rope

First stars (12,800) .... 6' 7" from the start of rope

Earth (4,600) .... 66' 5" from the start of rope

Oceans (3,800) .... 72' 3" from the start of rope

Prokaryotes (3,600) .... 73' 9" from the start of rope

Oxygen atmosphere (3,150) .... 77' from the start of rope

Eukaryotes (1,500) .... 89' from the start of rope

Cambrian "explosion" (545) .... 96' from the start of rope

Vertebrates (fish) (475) .... 96' 6" from the start of rope

Land animals (millipedes) (420) .... 97' from the start of rope

Amphibians (325) .... 97' 7" from the start of rope

Reptiles (250) .... 98' 4" from the start of rope

Mammals (200) .... 98' 6" from the start of rope

Death of dinosaurs (65) .... 5 5/8" from end

Primates (50) .... 4 3/8" from end

Ancestor of chimpanzees and hominids (16) .... 1 3/8" from end

Hominids (7) .... 5/8" from end

Lucy (4.5) .... 3/8" from end

Harnessing fire (0.75) . . . . 1/16" from end

Neanderthals (0.2) . . . . too close to mark (.02")

Homo sapiens sapiens (0.05) . . . . too close to mark (.0044")

Invention of writing (0.006) . . . . too close to mark (.0005")

Jesus' birth (0.002) . . . . too close to mark (.0002")

Science's birth (0.0016) . . . . too close to mark (.0001")

*Million years ago

Set of volumes
(30 books, 500 pages per book, 915 words per page)

Big Bang (13,700*) . . . . First word on the first page

First stars (12,800). . . . . Almost at the end of Book 2

Earth (4,600). . . . . Almost at the end of Book 20

Oceans (3,800) . . . . Midway through Book 22

Prokaryotes (3,600). . . . . Early in Book 23

Oxygen atmosphere (3,150) . . . . Early in Book 24

Eukaryotes (1,500) . . . . Three-quarters through Book 27

Cambrian "explosion" (545) . . . . Near the end of Book 29

Vertebrates (fish) (475) . . . . At the end of Book 29

Land animals (millipedes) (420). . . . . At the beginning of Book 30

Amphibians (325) . . . . Book 30, page 560

Reptiles (250). . . . . Book 30, page 642

Mammals (200) . . . . Book 30, at the beginning of page 697

Death of dinosaurs (65) . . . . Book 30, page 844

Primates (50) . . . . Book 30, page 861

Ancestor of chimpanzees and hominids (16) . . . . Book 30, page 898

Hominids (7) . . . . Book 30, page 908

Lucy (4.5) . . . . Book 30, at the beginning of page 911

Harnessing fire (0.75). . . . . Book 30, top fifth of last page

Neanderthals (0.2) . . . . Book 30, next to last paragraph

Homo sapiens sapiens (0.05) . . . . Book 30, last paragraph

Invention of writing (0.006) . . . . Book 30, next to last sentence

Jesus' birth (0.002). . . . . Book 30, last sentence

Science's birth (0.0016) . . . . Book 30, last sentence

*Million years ago

Evolution Dialogues

The cosmic day (24 hours)

Big Bang (13,700*) . . . . On the strike of midnight
First stars (12,800) . . . . Just before 2 a.m.
Earth (4,600) . . . . Just before 4 p.m.
Oceans (3,800) . . . . 5:20 p.m.
Prokaryotes (3,600) . . . . 5:45 p.m.
Oxygen atmosphere (3,150) . . . . 6:30 p.m.
Eukaryotes (1,500) . . . . 9:20 p.m.
Cambrian "explosion" (545) . . . . Just after 11:00 p.m.
Vertebrates (fish) (475) . . . . 11:10 p.m.
Land animals (millipedes) (420) . . . . 11:15 p.m.
Amphibians (325) . . . . 11:25 p.m.
Reptiles (250) . . . . 11:35 p.m.
Mammals (200) . . . . 11:40 p.m.
Death of dinosaurs (65) . . . . 11:53 p.m.
Primates (50) . . . . 11:55 p.m.
Ancestor of Chimpanzees and Hominids (16) . . . . 11:58 p.m.
Hominids (7) . . . . 45 sec before midnight
Lucy (4.5) . . . . 28 sec before midnight
Harnessing fire (0.75) . . . . 5 sec before midnight
Neanderthals (0.2) . . . . 1 sec before midnight
Homo sapiens sapiens (0.05) . . . . 1/2 sec before midnight
Invention of writing (0.006) . . . . 40/1,000 sec before midnight
Jesus' birth (0.002) . . . . 13/1,000 sec before midnight
Science's birth (0.0016) . . . . 1/1,000 sec before midnight

Million years ago

Index

A

Accommodation, principle of, 44

Adaptive traits, 30, 54, 55, 56

Addams, Jane, 83

Advancement of Learning, The (Bacon), 42

Agassiz, Louis, 77, 81

Agnostic, 79

AIDS, 57

Alleged "controversy" over evolution, 154

Alone in the World? (van Huyssteen), 171

"Alternative theories to evolution", teaching, 154

American Association of Physical Anthropologists, 164

American Civil Liberties Union (ACLU), 90, 158

Ammonite, 21

Amphibians, 140

Analogies, 136

Animals, arrival of, 138–141

Annals of the World (Ussher), 38, 39

Anning, Mary, 20

Archaea, 131

Archetypes, 76

Argument from design, 42

Arthropods, 138, 140

Asian religions, response to Darwin's theory, 87

Assumptions, mathematical, 123

Astrobiology, 70

Athanasius, Saint, 116

Atheist, 79

Augustine of Hippo (Saint Augustine), 41–42, 84, 116

Axioms, mathematical, 123

B

Bacon, Francis, 42

Bacteria, 131

Barbour, Ian, 170

Barth, Karl, 168

Beagle, H.M.S., 28–29, 31, 60, 76, 77, 131

Behe, Michael, 160–161

Bible, 37, 115, 116, 117, 118, 125

    the Bible according to Galileo, 42

    book of Genesis, 38, 39–40, 44, 45, 46, 156

    historical nature of the, 44–45

    King James version, 38

    New Testament, 40, 44, 115

    Old Testament, 38, 39, 40, 44, 115

    Pentateuch, 44

    seamless blending of knowledge, 38–39

    translations, 124

    the world as inferred from the, 39–40

Biblical inerrancy, 86, 125–126

Biblical infallibility, 126

Big Bang Theory, 137

Biogeographers, 67

Birds, 140, 141

Bohr, Niels, 105

Book of Nature, 41

Book of Scripture, 41

Bryan, William Jennings, 90–91

Buckland, William, 44

C
Calvinist Protestantism, 39
Cambrian explosion, 138–139
Carnegie, Andrew, 83
Cells, 62–63
Chambers, Robert, 74, 76
Chapman, John "Johnny Appleseed," 52
Chloroplasts, 138
Christ, 118
Christianity, 35–37
 the Bible, 38–40, 44–45
 Christian belief and history, 118–120
 the Christian story, 118
 contested knowledge, 124–126
 contexts of knowing, 121
 Darwin's religious views, 47–48
 defining, 114
 defining religion, 122–123
 evolving Christian responses to Darwin's theory, 84–86
 evolving sense of history, 44–47
 faith as the starting point, 123–124
 foundations of, 115–117
 fundamentalist, 87–88, 156
 natural philosophy and natural theology, 41–44
 1960s Christian fundamentalists movement, 157
 scientists and Christians, 177–179
Christian Natural Theology, A (Cobb), 172
Chromosomes, 104
Classification system for organisms, 21–22
Cobb, John, 172
Co-evolution, 69, 129
Combustion theory, 167
Complex specified information, 160
Constantine (Roman emperor), 119
Contemporary stances toward evolution, 149–152
 creation and evolution as complementary, 168–170
 creation and evolution as interactive, 170–172
 "intelligent design," 158–167
 "scientific" creationism, 156–158
 a touchy subject, 153–155
Continental drift theory, 104
Convergent evolution, 136
Copernicus, 42, 117
Creation and evolution
 as complementary, 168–170
 as interactive, 170–172
Creationism, "scientific," 156–158
Creationism, "young-earth," 156
Creation Research Society, 156

Creation and the World of Science (Peacocke), 171
Creeds, 120
Crustaceans, 103
Cultural evolution, 145–146
Cuvier, Georges, 21–22, 25, 77

D
Darrow, Clarence Seward, 90–91
Darwin, Annie, 47
Darwin, Charles, 26, 28–33, 38, 43. See also Responses to Darwin's theory
 religious views, 47–48
 theory of evolution, 32–33, 38, 50–51, 54, 59–60, 62, 63, 65, 67, 97–98, 102–103, 105, 131, 154, 155
Darwin, Emma Wedgwood, 47
Darwin, Erasmus, 26, 28, 47
Darwin, Robert, 28, 47
Darwin's Black Box (Behe), 160
Darwin on Trial (Johnson), 159
Data, scientific, 100
Day-age theory, 45, 157
Deep evolutionary time, 199–201
Degenerative depiction of evolution, 25–26
Dembski, William, 159–161
Denominations, 85, 120
Descent of Man, The (Darwin), 32
Descent with modification, 30, 54, 62, 65, 67, 155, 162–163
Dinosaurs, 140, 141
 dinosaur fossils, 65
Discovery Institute, 162
DNA, 55–56, 63, 131, 133–134, 137, 141
DNA sequence, 133
Dobzhasky, Theodosius, 19
Doctrines, religious, 120, 124

E
Earth
 Earth's age, 23–24, 45–46, 65–66
 succession of life on, 25–27
Earth Policy Institute, 147
Education
 debate over teaching evolution, 153–154
 "intelligent design," 158, 159, 162, 167
 public reaction against teaching evolution, 89
 "scientific" creationism in science curriculum, 157–158
 Scopes Monkey Trial, 90–91, 156, 158
Einstein, Albert, 105
Empirical evidence, 21, 47
Empirical inquiry, 122

Endosymbiosis, 138

Enlightenment, 115

Episcopal Church, "Catechism of Creation," 169–170

Essay on the Principle of Population, An (Malthus), 29

Essays and Reviews (Powell), 80

Euclid, 123

Eugenics, 83

Eukaryotes, 138

Evangelical Christians, 85–86

"Evidence for and against" evolution, 154

Evolution. *See also* Responses to Darwin's theory; Theory of evolution
    anti-evolution laws, 91
    co-evolution, 69, 129
    convergent, 136
    cultural, 145–146
    Darwin's avoidance of term "evolution," 30
    first application to natural history, 27
    future of, 145–147
    microevolution and macroevolution, 59–60, 161–162
    Scopes Monkey Trial, 90–91, 156, 158
    Social Evolution, 83
    theistic, 81

Evolutionary developmental biology, 134–135

Evolutionary theology, 171

Evolutionary time (deep time), 199–201

Evolution and Dogma (Zahm), 84

Evolution vs. Creationism (Scott), 164

Experience, Christian knowledge and, 115, 116–117

Extinction, evidence of, 21–22

F

Fables, 99

Facts, scientific, 100, 163

Faith of a Physicist, The (Polkinghorne), 171

Final Cause, 76

Finding Darwin's God (Miller), 164

First Cause, 26, 48, 76

First Principles (Spencer), 27

FitzRoy, Robert, 28, 77

Flood geology, 156

Fossils, 46, 52, 64–65, 66, 67
    fossil-finders, 20–21
    transitional, 63–64

Foundation for Thought and Ethics, 159

Freethinkers, 26, 47

Fundamentalist Christianity, 87–88, 156

"Fundamentals: A Testimony to the Truth, The," 87–88

Fungi, 132

G

Galapagos Islands, 29, 30, 59–60, 67, 79

Galileo Galilei, 42, 117, 125, 168

Galton, Francis, 83

Gap theory, 46, 157

Gene pool, 56, 59

Genes, 133

Genesis Flood, The (Morris and Whitcomb), 156, 157

Genetic drift, 58–59

Genetics
    decoding genetic information, 134
    development of the field of, 33
    Mendelian, 33, 102

Genus, 142–143

Germ theory, 95, 167

God After Darwin (Haught), 172

God of the Gaps position, 159

Gompers, Samuel, 83

Goodfriend, Glenn A., 64

Gospel, 118

Gould, Stephen Jay, 64, 168

Grant, Peter and Rosemary, 60

Gray, Asa, 80–81

"Great chain of being" doctrine, 22, 40

H

Haught, John, 122, 172

Heat flow theory, 65–66

Hefner, Philip, 171

Higher criticism, 44

HIV virus, 57, 145

Hominins, 141–142, 171

Hominoid species, 62

Homologies, 43, 63, 136

Hooker, Joseph, 32, 79

Human Factor, The (Hefner), 171

Human fossils, 65

Human origins, 141–145

Human Phenomenon, The (Teilhard), 170–171

Hutton, James, 23, 24

Huxley, Thomas Henry, 72–73, 78–79, 81

Hypothesis, scientific, 97–98, 100, 102–103, 163

I

Igneous rock, 23, 24

Index of Forbidden Books, 84

Inductive reasoning, 42

Industrial Age, 45

Inherit the Wind (play), 91

Insects, 132, 140

Institute for Creation Research, 156
"Intelligent design," 158–163
    scientific arguments against, 164–167
Irreducible complexity, 160, 165–166
Islam, response to Darwin's theory, 86–87
Isotopic dating, 66, 134, 157
Issues in Science and Religion, 170

J
James ossuary, 114, 118
James, William, 121
John Paul II, Pope, 168–169
Johnson, Phillip, 159
Judaism, response to Darwin's theory, 86

K
Kingsley, Charles, 80
Kipling, Rudyard, 97
Koran, 86

L
Lamarckian cultural evolution, 146
Lamarck, Jean-Baptiste, 26–27, 82
Laws of inheritance, 33
Leclerc, Georges Louis (Comte de Buffon), 21, 23, 25–26
Leo XIII, Pope, 84
Life
    arrival of plants and animals, 138–141
    life's origins, 136–138
    succession of, 25–27
Linnaeus, Carl, 21
List of Forbidden Books, 84
Liturgies, 120
Local, adaptive radiation, 67
Luther, Martin, 116
Lyell, Charles, 23–24, 29, 32, 77–78

M
Macroevolution, 60, 161–162
Magisteria, 168
Mainline churches, 169
Mainline denominations, 85
Malthus, Thomas, 29
Mammals, 133, 140, 141
Material reductionists, 108
Mathematical assumptions, 123
Mendel, Gregor, 33, 102
Messiah, 118
Metazoa, 138
Meteorological theory, 167

Methodological naturalism, 107
Microbes, 131–132
Microevolution, 59–60, 161–162
Miller, Kenneth, 164, 165
Minnesota schools, evolution debate in, 153–154
Mitochondria, 138
Modern synthesis, 33, 102
"Monkey-to-man" question, 75
Morris, Henry, 156, 157
Muslims, response to Darwin's theory, 86–87
Mutations, 55, 57, 133–134
Mystery of Life's Origins, The, 158–159

N
National Center for Science Education, 164
Natural History Magazine, 168
Natural philosophers, 41–42
Natural selection, 31, 32, 47–48, 54–57, 82, 155
Natural theology, 42–44
Natural Theology (Paley), 42–43
Newton, Isaac, 178
"Nonoverlapping magisteria," 168

O
Of Pandas and People (Davis, Kenyon), 159, 164
Ontological naturalism, 108
Organic succession, 25, 46
Origins of life, 136–138
Origin of Species, The (Darwin), 32, 50–51, 69, 72–73
    backlash towards, 87–89
    enthusiastic support for, 78–81
    evolution of scientific and public opinion, 81–83
    evolving Christian responses to, 84–86
    qualified acceptance of, 77–78
    rejection of, 75–77
    response from other religions, 86–87
    science and, 97, 102
    as topic of personal interest, 74–75
Ossuary, 114, 118
Our Family Tree (Peters), 153–154
Owen, Richard, 29, 43, 76, 81

P
Paleoanthropologists, 141, 171
Paley, William, 42–43, 160
Peacocke, Arthur, 171
Peters, Lisa Westberg, 153
Philanthropists, 83
Philosophie Zoologique (Lamarck), 27
Photosynthesis, 138

Phyla, 139
Phylogenetic diagrams, 134, 135
Phylogeny, 134
Planck, Max, 105
Plants and animals, arrival of, 138–141
Plesiosaurus, 20
Polkinghorne, John, 171
Powell, Rev. Baden, 80
Presbyterian Church (USA), 2002 resolution, 169
Primates, 141
Principle of accommodation, 44
Principles of Geology (Lyell), 24, 29
Process theology, 172
Prokaryotes, 138
Protestantism, Calvinist, 39
Protists, 132
Public Broadcasting System (PBS), 167
Punctuated equilibrium, 68

Q
Quantum theory, 104–105

R
Radioactivity, 66
Reason, Christian knowledge and, 115
Recombination, 55, 133
Religion
    defining, 122–123
    historical, 118
Responses to Darwin's theory, 72–73
    buildup toward a backlash, 87–89
    enthusiastic support, 78–81
    evolution of scientific and public opinion, 81–83
    evolution on trial, 90–91
    evolving Christian responses, 84–86
    qualified acceptance, 77–78
    rejection, 75–77
    response from other religions, 86–87
    as topic of personal interest, 74–75
Revelation, 115
Revolutions (natural disasters), 22
Rites, 120
RNA, 63, 137
Roman Catholic Church
    Christian tradition in, 115–116
    and evolutionary theory, 168–169
    rejection of Darwin's theory, 76–77
    response to evolution, 84–85

S
Schmitz-Moormann, Karl, 171
Science
    defined, 98–99
    differences between religion and, 124
Science behind evolution, 93–96
    certainty and uncertainty, 103–105
    construction of knowledge about evolution, 102–103
    levels of scientific knowledge, 100–102
    non-scientific interpretations of science, 105–107
    what science is, 97–99
    what science is not, 107–108
"Scientific" creationism, 156–158
Scientific discovery, period of, 20–21
Scientific method, 101
Scientific theory, 100–101, 124, 155, 163
Scopes, John, 90–91
Scopes Monkey Trial, 90–91, 156, 158
Scott, Eugenie, 164
Sedgwick, Adam, 75–76
Sedimentary rock, 23–24
Sexual selection, 57–58
Sixth Extinction, 147
Smallpox, 57
Smith, Huston, 123
Social Darwinism, 83, 89
Social Evolution, 83
Sonleitner, Frank, 164
Sorcerer II (yacht), 131–132
Special creation, 39–40, 157
Speciation, 30
Species
    arrival of plants and animals, 138–141
    Cro-Magnons, 144–145
    defined, 60–62
    evolutionary inquiry about, 68–69
    Homo sapiens, 78, 87, 141, 143, 144, 145
    human origins, 141–145
    microbial, 131–132
    Neanderthals, 143–144, 145
    new species of monkey, 133
    Peking Man, 170–171
Spencer, Herbert, 27, 31, 83, 89
Steno, Nicolaus, 24
Strata, rock, 23, 24, 25
Succession of life, 25–27
Sumner, William Graham, 83, 89
Sun-centered universe, 42
Supreme Court, U.S., 157, 158
"Survival of the fittest," 31, 83, 89

T

Taylor, Frank, 104

Teilhard de Chardin, Pierre, 170–171

"Temple of Nature, The" (E. Darwin), 26

Tetrapods, 140

Theistic evolution, 81

Theology of Creation in an Evolutionary World (Schmitz-Moormann), 171

Theory of the Earth, The (Hutton), 23

Theory of evolution. *See also* Responses to Darwin's theory

    Darwin's, 32–33, 38, 50–51, 54, 59–60, 62, 63, 65, 67, 97–98, 102–103, 105, 131, 154, 155

    evidence for evolution, 62–67

    evolution in action, 52–54

    focus of current research, 67–70

    microevolution and macroevolution, 59–62

    natural selection, 54–57

    other evolutionary mechanisms, 57–59

Thomas Aquinas, Saint, 116

Thompson, William (Lord Kelvin), 65–66

Traditions, Christian, 115–116

Transitional fossils, 63–64

Transmutation, 27

"Tree of life"

    emergence of species creating a, 62

    evolution depicted as, 54

Trilobites, 65

Trinity, 119

Triumph of an Idea, The (PBS), 167

Tuberculosis, 145

U

Uniformitarianism, 24

Unitarian, 47

Use inheritance, 27

Ussher, James, 38–39

V

Van Huyssteen, Wentzel, 171

Varieties of Religious Experience, The (James), 121

Venter, J. Craig, 131–132

Vertebrates, 21, 22, 140

Vestiges of the Natural History of Creation (Chambers), 74, 76

Viruses, 131

W

Wallace, Alfred Russel, 32, 78

Warfield, B. B., 86

Wegener, Alfred, 104

"What Every Theologian Should Know About Creation, Evolution, and Design" (Dembski), 159–160

"What's Wrong with Pandas?" (Sonleitner), 164

Whitcomb, John C., 156, 157

Wilberforce, Samuel (Bishop of Oxford), 72–73, 76, 81

World as explained by evolution, 127–130

    arrival of plants and animals, 138–141

    diversity beyond measure, 131–133

    future of evolution, 145–147

    human origins, 141–145

    life's origins, 136–138

    one big family, 133–136

Worldview, 105–106

World War I, 89

Y

Young-Earth creationism, 156

Z

Zahm, Father John, 84

Zoonomia, or, the Laws of Organic Life (E. Darwin), 26